A DOG LIKE RALPH

A book for anyone who has ever loved a rescue dog...

CLARE COGBILL

A Dog Like Ralph

Revised July 2013
ISBN 1479220256
ISBN-13: 9781479220250

I would like to dedicate this book to those who share my vision of a world without suffering, and those who give of their time willingly and altruistically to help people and animals in need.

Author's Note

When all three of our much loved, elderly dogs passed away within a year of one another, we were devastated. We had known they were all fading fast from a variety of ailments, but we hadn't expected them to leave us in such quick succession. When the last old gentleman of our three dogs, Oskar, died we felt a deep void and a sense of loss we knew could only be filled by finding ourselves another canine companion. All thoughts of remaining dog-less for a few months to enable us to 'go travelling' went out of the window when, just a few days after losing Oskar, I found myself desperately looking at animal shelter web pages trying to find the dog who would once again make our family complete.

The Internet has brought with it a new dawn in the search for an animal companion in that we no longer have to trawl along rows and rows of cages or kennels to find the animal we want to take home. Instead, we can look at regularly updated animal shelter websites, which contain galleries of homeless animals.

It was on one of these pages we discovered Ralph, who very quickly made his way onto our shortlist of 'dogs who would be likely to suit our lifestyle'.

Easy enough you would think, especially if you don't have to look directly into the eyes of the dogs you are rejecting, but there were so many who would have suited us that we finished up with a shortlist of over twenty. After much soul-searching, we eventually managed to reduce the list to just six. Ralph was 'number two' on that list and the one we ended up going to see, because on the morning we got in touch with staff at the shelter that had been caring for 'number one', the particular dog we liked had just an hour earlier been offered a home.

Sometimes these things turn out as they are meant to be, and you end up where you should be and with the ones you are destined to be with; and so, later on that day when we arrived at the kennels to meet number two, we were bowled over by him. He was the most handsome dog we had ever seen.

With his gangly long legs, big feet, oversized floppy ears and a mind full of mixed-up emotions about people, cars, roads, cats, the rain, rabbits and other dogs, Ralph came home with us to a life in which he would have to confront all of these things on a regular basis. We hadn't accounted, however, for his extreme reactions to these and other encounters, which were sometimes heartrending, sometimes extreme and sometimes comical.

Having had many dogs before, coupled with me being a qualified veterinary nurse, and with the bonus (or so we thought) of being a family who considered ourselves to be 'experienced dog owners' —we took on this crazy, nervous dog. A dog who turned out to be our biggest-ever canine challenge. On spending time with him, however, we very quickly realised that embedded in him was a fear that had been instilled by whatever he had been through before.

This is Ralph's story, as told by him, a couple of friends he meets along the way ... and me.

Spring

CHAPTER 1

Ralph

A sharp pain seared across my muzzle and I panicked. I pulled back and cowered, my whole body trembling with fear. Then came the retreat. I shrank further into the corner and tucked my head between my back legs, waiting for their return. The stinging pain continued as a warm fluid ran down my face. Suddenly I heard a voice in the distance, echoing, as it got louder and clearer, penetrating the air. Then I woke and looked around me, gradually taking in the sounds and smells of this new environment.

Okay.

I was okay.

I quickly did a body check as I scanned the area around me. The pain across my muzzle had eased. They walked in my direction and spoke to me—their voices didn't sound threatening; but even so, I cowered and trembled, pushing myself into the back corner. But they could still reach me. They spoke again, more softly this time. I glanced up at them and they seemed familiar, so I relaxed.

When a hand reached towards me, I shrank into a tight ball—until I caught the scent of something that smelt like food.

Then I remembered: this place was different.

Yes, the people were different here and, while it was noisy and people passed by all day long, when it got dark there came a calm peacefulness I hadn't known before. That was when I was able to nuzzle next to another dog; she would let me reach out and touch her feet with mine. I often woke up twitching during the night, but then eventually I would drift back to sleep. In time, I would see that morning had come and I was still in the safe place.

Each day was like the next, with gates being opened and closed, and people coming and going, and walking past me. One day my companion disappeared and, for a short time, I was alone. Then they brought in another dog, but he wasn't the same as my first companion, so he slept in his bed and I slept in mine. People came and people went. Dogs came and dogs went. Some dogs let me snuggle up against them, which really comforted me, while others growled and showed me their sharp, white teeth. I tried to stay out of their way, but all I really wanted was to play games with them or snuggle into their warmth.

Finally, a day came that was different from the one before. I cowered as a hand placed a loop around my neck. The person led me out of my familiar area and through the gate. I tried to pull back but she insisted. Reluctantly, I followed. Her hands offered me pieces of food, but I didn't eat any of them because I was too worried about what was going on around me.

What was happening? I wanted to know. Why wasn't she putting me in the run to play with the other dogs? I was led to a building I had never seen before, where people kept reaching out to touch my head. So many hands coming towards me made me nervous, so I backed away. My ear had turned inside out, so the person on the other end of the loop flipped it back the right way as she stroked my head and spoke softly.

We waited. I heard ringing sounds and talking. Then the one who had stroked my head passed the end of the loop to someone else and leaned towards me. She tried to touch my head with her face, but I backed away. When she touched my head again, her mouth made a sound, but I didn't understand. She walked back into the building; I was left outside with the other person and she, too, made sounds with her mouth. I listened carefully, wanting to under-stand. She reached out to me, but again I trembled. Curious, though, I watched her every move.

We walked to the back of a vehicle and one of them opened it. Someone patted her hand on what looked and smelt like a dog bed. I pulled away because I wanted to go back to my own bed with the growling dogs and my friends in the run who let me dance circles around them and play with their toys. But they insisted. Before I knew what was happening, one of them had lifted me into the back of the vehicle and put a few pieces of food down on the bed beside me.

Then, the door slammed.

I'd been there before, or it seemed as though I had. Soothing sounds drifted from the front of the vehicle. I curled comfortably into the softness of the bed and rocked to sleep as we moved along. I slept and dreamed of warmth and of nuzzling into the soft fur of the other dogs. I dreamed of chasing them around outside. Then the vehicle stopped and one of them leaned over from the front and passed another piece of food to me. I knocked it out of her hand and it fell in front of me. I backed away from the hand, not sure what was going on and, once more, my body began trembling. Food was the last thing on my mind.

When the door opened, I pulled away from them because they were making sounds with their mouths that I didn't understand, and the unfamiliar screeching noises of the other vehicles frightened me. One person leaned forward and checked the loop around my neck by pulling on it. When I backed away, he reached in further, putting his arms around me and helping me to the ground. I cowered to the floor, but he pulled me forward; I had no choice but to follow. I noticed someone else nearby, who didn't sound threatening, but that didn't stop me from looking for a way to make a quick escape. Guessing my intentions, he pulled tighter on the loop. I suddenly felt strong arms around me again, and then I was being lifted into another vehicle. What was going on? A rumble came from the front and we moved forwards.

Shortly after, I found myself in yet another vehicle. I knew right away when we stopped that this place was different, for I could smell other dogs. I relaxed as I heard them barking.

I felt safe again.

I was taken into a room in which people were all around me, crouching next to me, offering me pieces of food and a drink of water, but I was much more concerned with what was happening around me to bother with food. Pieces of paper were being shuffled above my head and I could hear ringing and strange sounds again. The person holding onto the loop gave it to someone else and reached down to speak to me, but I didn't know what he meant, so I pulled away from him. Then one of them ruffled my ears—I wasn't sure whether I liked it when people did that. Finally, the people who had taken me there left and I was alone in the room with the strange people who were making strange noises, and who were trying to touch me on my neck. Eventually, the door opened and someone walked me to another building, where she opened a gate and put me in an enclosure with another dog. The dog wagged her tail and seemed to like me.

I was happy.

The routine seemed the same as before. The people spoke gently to me like in the last place, but then I remembered the sharp pain on my muzzle and that something had hurt me before I had gone there; so each time the people approached me I tried to hide behind the other dogs. Somehow, though, they always managed to catch me with the loop. I made sure to keep an eye on them whenever they led me along a road, onto some grass, and for walks between the trees. I was often quite desperate to go to the toilet, so I went near the bushes. Once I was done, I moved quickly away. Sure enough, each time I left something on the grass, they reached into their clothes, pulled out a bag, and leaned forward to collect it. It was very strange behaviour indeed. Then they ruffled my ears. I had started to think that I liked it when they did that but couldn't help backing away from them. When they reached into their pocket again and offered me some food, I was too scared to eat it.

They let me off the loop in a big grassy area where there was another dog I had never seen before. The people were calling out a word that I'd heard before in the other place that was like this one. "Ralph!" they said, over and over again. I didn't know whether they were speaking to me or to the other dog, but I didn't care. I was too busy chasing him and running away when he chased me back. Every time they called out, "Ralph!" the other dog went over to them, so I imagined he was Ralph. When they called another name, "Moby," I figured that was me. Still, I carried on running around in the grassy area and, when they came near me, I ran away from them to search for a way out. But I couldn't find one. As they called out to me, I ran around and around in circles until I couldn't run anymore; I just wanted to get away. Eventually they cornered me, put the loop around my neck, and walked me back to the place where there was the other dog and my bed.

I was exhausted.

The days led into nights and back to days again, and sometimes I woke shaking as I recalled the pain across my face. Although things were better and the people seemed nice, I didn't trust them. Not after all that had happened before. When they came towards me with the loop, I always shied away from them. Then they would catch me, give me food, and we would go for a walk or onto the grass where I played with the other dogs.

Then, one morning they didn't bring me any food. Someone I didn't recognise came and placed the loop around my neck. He led me to another vehicle. I was scared. I wanted to go and play on the grass with the dog called Ralph, but this man bundled me into the vehicle. And there, in front of me, was another dog I'd not met before. He was wagging his tail and barking excitedly, but I didn't know why. "What a very strange dog," I thought to myself and turned my back to him.

After a short time, we stopped amid the sounds of other vehicles. The man opened the door and lifted the other dog out, but I cowered to the back of the cage and listened. I didn't know what was going on. I was scared, so I curled up, tucked my head between my back legs and wrapped my tail around my body. When the door opened again, the man caught hold of the loop attached to my neck and lifted me to the ground. I struggled, but I was forced to walk beside him.

Inside the building, I saw many people with dogs beside them. There were also people with cages, which contained creatures that glared at me from behind the bars. I had met some of those before, and because I knew they had sharp claws I kept my distance and avoided eye contact. I concentrated instead on trying to get away from the person with the loop that was around my neck. All I wanted was to get back to the place with the dog who let me snuggle into her fur. I noticed that the dog from the vehicle wasn't wagging his tail or barking anymore. He looked scared and he was making soft whimpering sounds. I was worried.

They took me through the doors to a room where there were other dogs, and more of those creatures with round, staring eyes and sharp claws, and they bundled me into a cage. I hurried to the back of it and pushed myself right up against the bars. One by one, the animals went through to another room. When they came back, they were either sleeping or crying, and some were howling. I shrank further into the cold, hard bars. When they came for me, I shrank even further, but it was no use. They led me out of the cage into an open area with strange smells. I smelt fear. I could also smell the fluid they put on the floor in the kennel that I shared with the other dog. Suddenly I felt a sharp pain in the back of my neck. When they put me back in the cage, I was relieved that it was over. But then my head started to feel heavy and everything looked foggy. In the distance, I heard the cage opening again, but I couldn't move. Something was happening, but I didn't know what. All I wanted to do was sleep.

Then there was nothing.

From far away I heard a dog whimpering. The sound got louder and closer. Then I realised it was me.

I howled as I felt the sharp pain cut across my muzzle. Then I remembered where I was, and the pain across my face was numbed as I felt another, much more throbbing pain between my hind legs. I drew my feet towards my head to protect myself. The back of my throat was dry and a little sore, and I was thirsty. Someone approached who opened the gate and reached in and stroked my head. I tried to move away from her, but my legs wouldn't let me stand up. I felt comforted by her soothing voice. She kept on saying "Ralph," which confused me.

The man from the other place came back, but I was feeling too wobbly and still sore between my legs to resist too much. The wound there smelt like the fluid that had run down my face that time before. I licked it, but that made it sting, so I decided to leave it alone. He lifted me into the cage that was in the vehicle and I saw the dog with the wagging tail, who was still not wagging it. He smelt just the same as I did. We both ended up back where we'd been that morning. I snuggled into my soft bed and slept for a very long time.

Over the days that followed, they kept on putting the loop around my neck and looking between my legs and saying, "Ralph," but I couldn't see him anywhere. Then they gave me bits of food and tried to touch my head. I wasn't falling for that one, so they took me for a walk through the trees with the other dog, who was also really wobbly on his hind legs. I understood how he felt.

Most days many people walked past the gate of the place where I slept, and sometimes the loop would be placed over my head. They would then take me out for a walk through the trees or onto the grassy area to play with other dogs, like that one named Ralph and another one I had met named 'Boo'. One day, the dog I was sharing a kennel with disappeared, and that afternoon they brought in another dog. He had black fur and was big and strong and, at first anyway, I was a little wary of him, but he turned out to be good fun. Sometimes I would reach out and touch his feet with my feet when I was lying down. He didn't mind; he just wagged his tail a lot. He didn't let me sleep in his bed with him, though, and nuzzle into his fur as my previous companion had. He sometimes sniffed the part between my legs that was sore, but I would sit down so he couldn't. One day, he didn't get any food in the morning and instead went away for the day. He came back later smelling of the place I had been. Then he, too, had a sore part.

One day my routine was broken. I had already been for my walk and had my breakfast, after which I would usually have taken a nap. However, when someone opened the gate, I hid behind my big companion, who was extremely excited and wagging his tail. In front of us were some people I had never seen before. Expecting the worst, I stayed behind my friend hoping the loop was for him instead of for me, but they place the loop around my neck, while my friend was pushed back into the kennel. I had to walk beside the people I had never met, who kept saying, "Ralph." I looked and

looked around for Ralph, but he was nowhere to
be seen. The one with the loop passed it to one
of the new people, and we went for a walk along
the path between the trees. They kept trying to
touch my head, but I was still unsure. Then a dog
who had never seemed to like me walked past with
someone. He barked and growled at me, so I was
glad when we turned and walked another way.

We walked between the trees and went around
more than once, which was nice, and then they took
me to sit next to a bench. I sat as far from them as
possible, but when they offered me pieces of food, I
inched a little closer. One of them tried to touch my
head, so I backed away. Another one of them put
out her hand for me to sniff, and then she touched
my cheek and neck and said, "Ralph." I relaxed a
little, even though I still couldn't see him anywhere.
They began talking to one another, and I hoped
they would forget that I was there. Eventually they
led me towards the building and spoke to the people with the loops. I was taken back to the kennel
where the big, happy dog was waiting for me, wagging his tail. I was pleased to see him again.

Later on that night, I woke shaking. I could feel
the pain searing across my face again. Frightened,
I looked around me. Nearby, the big, happy dog
was sleeping. Deep rumbling sounds were coming out of his mouth, and his lips were moving as
he breathed in and out. I relaxed and sighed as I
reached my paws towards him and closed my eyes.

The next morning, the routine was the same.
After we had eaten all our food, the big dog and I
went out for a walk alongside the trees, where I went

to the toilet and they gave me a piece of food. We went back to the kennel and the mess that the big black dog had left there in the night had gone, and the floor smelt like the place where I hurt between my legs. Ready for a nap, I lay down on my bed to go to sleep. I was just drifting into a deep sleep when the gate opened and the loop appeared, so I scampered behind the big dog. They caught me instead and I couldn't get away. The big dog was trying to get out of the gate, too, but they shut it quickly behind me. He whined because he wanted to come for a walk, but I was so scared I couldn't focus on anything but what was happening to me.

We walked over to a nearby building and once inside I recognised the people who had been to see me before, and they had another dog with them. I looked down at the dog and she was so small. I sniffed her, and my tail came out from where I was hiding it between my legs. She sniffed me, too, so I jumped forwards to play with her. I guessed she wasn't in the mood for playing because she growled. So I tossed my head, and then she growled some more. Eventually she wagged her tail at me. We tried to jump around, but the loops prevented us from playing properly.

The people reached out and put something on the tight band around my neck, and I tried to escape, but the door was closed and there was nowhere to go. They said "Ralph" again, but he wasn't there, so I cowered and trembled, and the person holding the loop tried to touch my neck. I froze. The little dog was jumping up at me and wagging her tail, so I stood up straight and looked down at her. I couldn't believe how small she was. She raised her lips and showed me her sharp teeth, so I quickly looked away and ignored her. She had some attitude, that dog.

Once we got outside it was raining hard. I hated the rain, so all I wanted to do was go back inside. We walked near some trees towards a vehicle. The people put the little dog into the front of it. I got soaked as they tried to get me into the back, but all I wanted was to return to my kennel with the big dog and my warm bed.

CHAPTER 2

Us

Oskar was the last in a long succession of dogs—dogs I'd loved and lost since childhood.

Following a year of treatment for heart problems, he collapsed outside next door's house one warm, May morning on our way back from our slow amble around the block. No longer able to pump the blood to his limbs to enable him to stand, his heart had finally given up. He was still conscious, so I stayed by his side, stroking his head and talking to him softly while I waited for my son, Anthony, to bring a blanket so we could lift him back to our house.

Just a few weeks before, when I'd known in my heart that Oskar was beginning to struggle and that the pills—by then given to him at the highest possible dose—weren't helping him as much as they had been, I'd whispered into his ear for him to let me know when his time had come. All I had wanted was some indication from him that the time was right, and I guess I knew that this was it. He couldn't have given me a stronger signal that he'd had enough of this world and that it was time for him to go.

Not being the best with other dogs, in that he was 'food aggressive', Oskar had never been an easy dog and had given us twelve years of what I suppose most dog behaviourists would call "managing the situation." In other words, no matter how hard you try, some dogs have such ingrained problems from their past that cannot be resolved, and so you just get on with things and cope with what you have. He was one of those difficult dogs who would never completely recover from the anxieties of the years before we had him, but we loved him unconditionally, and for the last few months of his life, he had been our only dog. We felt we had owed that to him when the other dogs from our multi-dog household had passed away. I hope that he enjoyed that time being the sole focus of our attention. I admit that we were tempted to find him a 'friend', but we had known deep in our hearts that he was happier on his own, and that he deserved some peace in his retirement.

Three months before Oskar died, we had lost Charlie, a liver and white (and rather temperamental) Border collie who had been with us for just a couple of years. Because he had fractured one of his front legs and had to have it amputated, we were known locally as "the people with the three-legged collie." My brother had adopted Charlie twelve years earlier after I'd been involved in this poor dog's treatment for massive injuries he had sustained when some awful person had thrown him from a moving car.

We'd all done everything we could to make Charlie's life a good one, and my brother had loved him but wasn't able to keep him any longer once Charlie had lost his leg. He lived in a first-floor maisonette and Charlie could no longer manage the stairs. My brother was very sick and on kidney dialysis by then, too, so we took Charlie home with us. Quite strangely, for such a temperamental dog, he fitted in well with Oskar and our other dog, Dillon. Still, never quite recovering from the trauma of his previous experiences, he was sometimes aggressive towards strangers.

Once again, as so many owners do, we found ourselves managing the situation. Whenever people came to visit, we'd put him in the back sitting room until they'd gone, along with a giant-sized dog chew to keep him occupied. His aggression was unlike any other dog I had ever dealt with, though, because when out on walks and off the lead he wouldn't bother with anyone or anything. He was so focused on getting from A to B—or collecting sticks (the larger the branch, the better, and he was often seen dragging what looked like half a tree behind him). Perhaps at home he was in some way defending his territory and the few people he actually did like!

Along with the food-aggressive lurcher, Oskar, and the people-aggressive collie, Charlie, by comparison, Dillon was the most even-tempered, wonderful dog who was so easy to care for and fitted so well into our family. He was very much Anthony's dog and a mongrel—a genuine mix of breeds full of the characteristic hybrid vigour common to crossbreeds. He really was the most wonderful dog any parent could ever want as a canine companion for their child. We got him the same year as we got Oskar, back in 2000, and my only regret is that we hadn't known him for his whole life. He was four and a half when we got him, and he really was the most placid-natured dog. Of all the dogs I have ever known and loved, Dillon was the one whom I would have relished the opportunity to have sat down with and had a cup of tea and a chat. He had all-knowing eyes and a sense of understanding all there was to know about the human species; it was as though he understood everything that was going on around him.

We had brought Dillon home to live with us, Oskar, and our other dog Jack. Dillon was happy doing whatever Anthony wanted and going wherever we wanted to go, and he expected (and got) everything he wanted in return. Anthony was just eleven years old when we took Dillon home from the dog shelter, and we had him for ten years until he developed terrible digestive problems that we tried to treat. But he was getting very old, and it was hard for him. Eventually, in addition to digestive problems, he became completely blind and deaf, by which time he had lost so much weight and his muscles had long since wasted to mere slivers. With each day, we knew that his time had come, or was very near.

One Sunday evening about a year before Oskar died, I walked through the hallway past the sitting room and glanced in. Dillon was standing in the middle of the room clearly not knowing what was going on or where he was. I walked in and touched the side of his cheek, at which he jumped, and I stayed beside him and talked to him, even though I knew he couldn't hear me or see me. I just hoped that feeling my hand caressing his ears gave him some comfort. I knew then that he'd had enough of life, and he was frightened. I guess, in my heart, I had known this for a few weeks, ever since he had started bumping into the furniture and the other two dogs.

Feeling sick in the pit of my stomach, I knew that the following morning we had a huge decision to make as a family. Bob and I could not get to sleep that night, and talked for hours about what we were going to do. The next day the three of us agreed we should arrange for the local vet to come to the house. We moved Dillon's bed, with him still in it, down to the sunroom. While we waited for the vet to arrive, we all lay next to him, talking to him and comforting him; meanwhile, we cried for the impending loss of this glorious creature.

When Dillon had come to join our family, we already had Oskar and another lurcher, Jack. Oskar had come into our lives when some friends of ours realised they couldn't cope with his aggression towards other dogs. We had brought him to live with us thinking we could cure him of it, anticipating that we had some miracle cure. We didn't and, as I said before, we managed the situation, which wasn't always easy. Though Oskar loved all of us, he formed a very special bond with Bob, and so he became 'his' dog. 'My' dog was Jack.

I have heard it said that if you choose to share your life with dogs, then at some point there would be one dog who comes along who takes over your whole being and becomes a part of you like no other. For me, that dog was Jack and, without taking anything away from the other dogs I have loved in the past, love now, and will love dearly in the future, Jack was like a shining star to me. I don't know what it is that makes a particular dog so special—perhaps the dog needs some extra nurturing, or maybe the dog nurtures you when you most need to be looked after. All I know for sure is that Jack was there by my side through some of the darkest times of my life.

I was on kidney dialysis and dialysing at home on a machine through the night. Each evening, once I had attached myself to the machine, Jack would come and lie by my side. He remained there through each night, pushing his body against my legs, and there he stayed until I woke. When I stirred in the middle of the night, I would lie on my side staring at the machine as it bleeped and chugged rhythmically while it kept me alive. While Bob slept behind me, Jack nuzzled my hand to let me know he was still there—all the time taking care of me.

Dillon and Jack adored each other. People say that threes don't always work and, whether that is true or not, times were occasionally difficult because of Oskar not being the easiest of dogs to manage. Eventually, though, everything seemed to settle into place and we all got on with our lives, work, and Anthony with school. They were a generation of dogs in a family who adored all of them and who each had special places in our hearts.

Jack eventually developed an aggressive form of nasal tumour and I lost him so suddenly when he was just ten years old. When your animals get old, or you know they are suffering from a chronic, terminal illness, you are able to prepare yourself in some ways for losing them. Eventually you see that their quality of life has diminished as they become very sick, and there's a sense of preparation for your impending grief. This all happens gradually and so, if necessary, you can make the decision to end their suffering after many months, or sometimes years, of anticipating that loss. With Jack, I had no time to prepare; he was diagnosed, and within three weeks, he had died. When I lost him, I lost a part of myself.

He had seen me through my dialysis treatment and stuck around for a year after my kidney transplant to make sure I was okay. Then, that was it—he was gone. I had loved him from the time we went searching for a companion for our old dog, Fluke, and his dark brown, velvet eyes had marked every step I took down the corridor at the rescue kennels. It was as though his eyes were penetrating something deep inside me, and I had known instinctively that he was the one.

It was therefore the eventual loss of Oskar and his contemporaries, Dillon and Charlie, that led to our living in a dog-less household. For me, this was the first time since I had grown up. It was the emptiness in our home, albeit for a short time, that led us to Ralph. Really, this story is mostly about him, as he epitomises so many things about rescue dogs and the ways in which they come to be where they are and why.

When I first set eyes on Ralph, I thought he was possibly the most handsome dog I had ever seen. He is a deep tan with clear, brilliant white markings, very unusual almond-shaped eyes, and the most incredibly floppy ears, which don't exactly complement what you would expect from his head and body shape. It would be more apt for him to have greyhound ears, but when you take his ears, his eyes, and his body, and place them together in the combination that is Ralph, somehow it works. When he walks, he trots (and it's a real trot, just like a horse), and when he approaches people when we are out walking, his antics make them smile. I've never seen that reaction in so many people. Yes, you get people like me who smile and say hello to every dog who walks past, but Ralph provokes that reaction in a good eighty or ninety percent of people who pass by —even those without dogs.

Having spent a few days without a dog in the house, we started looking at rescue centre websites within a hundred-mile radius of our home. Perhaps I should clarify that *I* started looking at websites, while Bob and Anthony, probably quite rightly, said it was too soon for us to get another dog. However, I had not been in a dog-less household for decades and so, defiantly, I went on to create a short list. The dog at the top of the short list was not Ralph, but another lurcher-type dog who was in a rescue shelter about eighty miles away; however, when I phoned about him, he'd just been offered a home. When we returned to our list, we saw the picture of

Ralph—the dog with the crazy ears—our 'number two'. We phoned the rescue shelter immediately and made arrangements for later that day to go to the kennels to meet him.

In hindsight, I am so glad that the other dog had found a home. From his description, he had sounded like a nice, calm, well-rounded, obedient dog. I guess my initial reaction when we had lost Oskar and Charlie had been to try to make our lives easier for a little while, and then maybe take on a more problematic dog later on as a companion for whichever dog we took. But that's not the way it worked out. I think sometimes that that is how things are; they simply turn out just the way they are supposed to be.

Our first glimpse of Ralph was as he hid behind a huge, black Labrador called Jed. Jed was boisterous and extremely friendly. One of the kennel assistants expertly manoeuvred him out of the way so she could slip the lead around Ralph's neck. With a great deal of reluctance, he walked beside us as we headed for the gate at the end of the covered corridor. Then we were out in the courtyard, where at last we were able to see him properly for the first time.

The picture from the website had not done him justice. He was also slightly larger than we had thought he was going to be. What the two-dimensional image on the web page also hadn't shown was the deep scar across his muzzle. It was about an inch and a half in length and perhaps gave some clue as to his extreme nervousness—something which no picture could ever have depicted. He flinched each time we reached out to touch him, and only when we took the lead to take him for a walk did he reluctantly follow us. As we wandered along beside him, he watched us, suspiciously marking every move we made with those gorgeous, dark brown, almond-shaped eyes.

We had been given some treats to help us make friends with him, and we spent some time walking him and talking to him, desperately trying to gain his confidence. When we had exhausted the walks available at the rescue centre, we sat on a bench on the grass near to where we had parked the car, and coaxed him some more. While he didn't actually take the treats from us, he came close enough to knock them out of our hands by snuffling them with the end of his nose and then picking them up from the floor. We all immediately fell hopelessly in love with him and wanted to take care of him. We longed to nurture him in an effort to restore his faith in people and this horrible world that had made him behave in this way.

If he would let us.

On our way home, we considered what we would call him. We thought of various names, one of which was Thor, the Norse god. We felt that by giving him the name of the God of Thunder, it would help him to grow in confidence. In the end, however, it all came back to Ralph, as Ralph just suits him. He has a face he pulls that makes him look like an old man. It is quite an old-fashioned name and you don't really hear of so many Ralphs these days, and certainly not dogs named Ralph.

We arranged to go back to see him the following day, with a view to being able to take him home, but first we had to introduce him to my mother's little dog, Luella. Now and then they would need to spend time together, so part of the deal had to be that he would get on with her. Luella is a Chihuahua crossed with a Jack Russell terrier (perhaps a little bit of corgi in there?) whom my mother had homed from the same kennels just weeks before.

Luella has the traits of both Chihuahuas and Jack Russell terriers, which is fortunate in some ways in that she is extremely loyal and protective, but not in others, as she suffers from that small-dog syndrome that many small dogs suffer from. When they look so much like babies do, with their large eyes and cute features, it is inevitable that so many small dogs become spoilt and end up trying to be in charge! That being said, however, Luella is rather a sweetie.

The following day when she met Ralph—and, quite characteristically, grumbled at him—he simply ignored her attempts to dominate and wanted to play with her. It was then we first saw the great potential that Ralph had as a pet dog. If he could behave like that when other dogs were around, then perhaps there was some inkling of a chance that he would also eventually behave like that with people.

Once all the paperwork was completed, per-suading Ralph to jump into the car in the pouring rain on the day we collected him was difficult, but eventually he leaped inside when we offered him a treat. He also seemed to weigh the benefits of sitting in a warm, dry car against hesitating in the downpour and getting soaking wet. Luella was in the front with us, and I think that maybe her being in the car helped Ralph to feel a little more at ease;

we had already realised that he was much happier in the presence of another dog.

On leaving the kennels, and knowing that we were used to having more than one dog, the staff had asked whether we would be getting another one to keep him company. In the weeks since they'd been looking after him, they had observed on many occasions how his whole attitude altered when other dogs were around, almost as though it enabled him somehow to forget his deep-seated fears. As a result, our intention to find him a companion delighted them. For a while, though, we knew we just needed to focus on Ralph.

Our hair and clothes dripping from the heavy summer rain, we headed home with two soggy dogs in the car. A sense of just a little trepidation hung in the air as this dog with the gorgeous almond-shaped eyes—which I now realised were framed at his eyelids with ginger eyelashes, and along the bottom of his eyes with thick brown 'eyeliner'—shrank into the depths of the back of the car, and was clearly extremely frightened. As I turned around in the car to talk to him about all those daft things you find yourself talking to your dog about, what became evident very quickly was his excessive use of calming signals. He yawned constantly whenever I looked his way or tried to stroke him, and he repeatedly licked his lips and averted his eyes from my gaze.

Calming signals, which dogs use to indicate how they are feeling and that they are not a threat to other animals, are a means of communicating without sound. In much the same way that people communicate with each other, the majority of communication in dogs is through body language. Specifically, calming signals are aspects of body language such as turning away, turning their head, sniffing the ground, yawning, excessive stretching, licking their lips or smacking them together, lifting a paw, and sitting. The signals also include urinating when approached by someone or something threatening, which most owners would immediately recognise as submissive or fearful behaviour. Less obvious signals include moving in an arc around another dog. Dogs usually use these signals on approach to another dog, and a trained eye will notice them. Many people will assume that if a dog yawns, then he is tired and, while this may be the case in some circumstances, it is often so, so much more than that.

Recognising Ralph's signals, I felt a feeling of dread deep in my abdomen. I had inadvertently brought an extremely troubled dog into our already hectic lives. While I did not regret the decision we had made, I felt distraught at what this poor dog must have endured to have made him behave in such a way. Part of his training was going to involve our letting him know that we weren't a threat to him; so, with no time being quite like the present, I set to work by giving him dog-style calming signals by licking my lips, yawning at him and avoiding his gaze. Amazingly, in spite of the huge amount of stress he was experiencing, within minutes of using the signs back at him, I sensed him beginning to relax. Using calming signals in this way to calm dogs who are nervous or aggressive can help the dog to feel much less anxious.

I realised that our work would be cut out for us over the coming months.

CHAPTER 3

Ralph

I finally gave in when I realised they had treats. They had smelt so good and the small dog was in the front looking back at me, eating one they had given her. I was soaking wet and the fluffy bed underneath me was soggy too. The person in front of me was talking to me and kept on saying, "Ralph," repeatedly. I was starting to think that perhaps they were having me on; I hadn't seen him for days. The sounds they were making were soothing, but I didn't know what they meant, so I was scared. I had left the big, black dog behind; he had made me feel safe. I was on my own with these strange people who had the loop, and this small dog who kept on showing her teeth to me.

As we moved along, I saw lots of grass and water, and I remembered running and chasing. I wasn't sure where they were taking me. Eventually we stopped, and they opened the car and placed the loop around my neck. I could smell so many different scents in the air that I did not recognise. They wanted me to jump out, so they called, "Ralph!" I jumped out because I thought that maybe he was there, but then they took me through a door and led me into a room. I sniffed around. I smelt the scent of the small dog, and when I looked down, there she was jumping up and down in front of me. She wasn't showing me her teeth anymore. They removed the loop that was attached to the tight collar that was around my neck, and they tried to get me to follow them. The woman reached forward. "Ralph," she said, as she touched my ear. I backed away. As they approached again, I licked my lips and yawned and turned my head to the side, but I could see from the corners of my eyes that they were still there looking at me.

The small dog with the teeth came running past me and I forgot the people and chased her through the room that smelt of food. I followed her outside. She kept glancing back at me, teasing me, tormenting me, so I followed her some more. Suddenly I caught the scent of something and had to relieve myself. Then, from not far away I heard someone say, "Good boy, Ralph!" I was confused, but I had this idea developing in my head that I might have been Ralph, too, or perhaps that was the name of the little dog who was running back into the building? So I followed her, and as I did so, the mat just inside the door went skidding across the floor and I nearly fell. I managed to remain upright and then continued chasing the dog up some stairs. "Luella! Ralph!" the people were saying, and so the small dog ran back down the stairs to them.

I chased her.

When I saw the people again, I stopped in my tracks and tried to find a way to escape, but the door by the mat was closed. They were all standing around me, but they were not trying to touch my head anymore. I sat down, yawned, licked my lips, and then turned my head away from them, but they were still looking at me and talking to me. By then the little dog was sitting next to them. I thought then that perhaps these people might have been okay. She seemed relaxed enough, and was even snuggled up next to them, watching me with those beady little eyes of hers.

They offered me a piece of food; I knocked it onto the floor with my nose, and then picked it up and gingerly nibbled at it. All the time I watched them to see what they were doing, but they just made noises that I didn't understand. One of them made a sound in my direction, but I just looked at her and stretched my legs out. I turned my head away and licked my lips. When I looked back, she was still there, so I yawned. Then she yawned back at me, licked her lips, and made a funny sound. As I looked at her from the corner of my eyes and reached forward with my toes, she did the same. But since she was a funny shape and not like me, I wasn't sure about her strange behaviour. I didn't think she would cause me any harm. When she pulled away from me without touching my head, I was relieved.

There was a soft bed on one side of the room, and one of them patted it with his hand and said, "Ralph." I thought that he must have been talking to me, so I walked over. A piece of food was there waiting for me. I looked back at him and yawned again; he yawned back at me. It seemed as though everything was okay, so I lay down and ate the food. I watched them constantly, though, just in case any of them made a sudden move.

The small dog was restless. The people spoke to her, but when I trotted over to stand by her, she leaped up next to where one of the people was sitting down. I had to look up at her because she was suddenly taller than I was. Then she raised her lips and showed me her teeth. I wasn't sure why she was being so unfriendly, so I felt a little afraid. Luckily for me, they put her on the floor and went out of the room for a short time; she followed them. They reappeared with a loop and attached it to the tight band around my neck. They put one on the band around the little dog with the teeth's neck too, and we headed out through the door. When I saw a lot of noisy vehicles passing, I took a few steps back inside, but the person who was holding the loop patted her leg and said something that included the word "Ralph," so I followed.

The dog with the teeth was marching along with her tail in the air, her superior attitude clear to anyone who was watching. I followed, as she obviously knew what she was doing and where we were going. All of the new smells interested me; some of them were intoxicating. We met another dog on a loop who had long, fluffy ears. When I went over to sniff her, she jumped up to my face. I bowed down on my front legs and tried to play, but the person holding onto her pulled her away. I had to go with the person who had my loop, so we followed the little dog with the teeth instead.

We took a path through some trees where I could smell many of those creatures with the long ears that reminded me of the time my face was hurt. I could smell them, but I couldn't see them. But I knew for sure they were there. The one who had the loop kept making sounds that I thought might be directed at me, but I wasn't sure. Since I didn't know what they meant, I looked the other way. We continued following the little dog. We spotted a dog like the big, happy dog I shared a kennel with before only he was much lighter. I wanted to play with him, but he didn't stop because the person who was with him put a loop around his neck and he walked on by. I glanced out of the corner of my eye, and yawned at him, while the little dog showed him her teeth and growled.

Shortly after we returned to the building, I was shown to the room that smelt of food. On the floor, there was a bowl on a stand and it was full of food, which I ate immediately because I was starving. I was also worried the dog with the teeth might have taken it if I didn't eat it, even though I wasn't sure whether she would be able to reach that high. After all, she had her own smaller bowl on a much smaller stand, so I don't think she would have stolen mine.

With a full stomach, I headed to the soft bed and lay down to sleep off the walk and the food. I tried to relax, but I couldn't because they kept on watching me. When they came near me and made noises, I didn't know what they wanted, so I leaned away from them and yawned. They yawned back, and I relaxed a little. I noticed that one of them was licking her lips and looking sideways at me, so I did the same. Reaching forward she touched my neck gently and made sounds and said, "Ralph." She went back and sat with the small dog and the other lady. The small dog seemed to be protecting that lady from something – I hoped it wasn't me, because I wouldn't hurt anyone. And then the one who was the biggest of them all came past and ruffled my ears. I backed away from him, but he said, "Ralph," and I was pretty sure by then that they meant me.

Later on, it was dark outside. One of the females came and attached the loop to the tight band around my neck and we headed out to where there were far fewer vehicles than there had been earlier. I followed the person with the small dog. She didn't seem to be as confident in the dark, but the dark didn't bother me. In fact, when I saw what was around the corner, I was beside myself with joy and started bounding around and pulling against the band around my neck; I was surrounded by a lot of those creatures that I had chased before, the ones with the big ears and the small, fluffy tails. So I leaped forward and pulled some more, but she held on tight. I tried to pull back but nearly slipped from the tight band around my neck. All I wanted was to go and chase those creatures, but they wouldn't let me.

We turned a corner and the creatures had gone, so I followed the dog with the teeth. We walked past places that had walls and hedges on one side and those places that the vehicles went along on the other. I caught whiffs of strong scents from tall posts with lights on them, and I could smell the dog who looked like the big, black friendly dog and the dog with the long ears. I could also smell the scent of a dog I hadn't yet met, who smelt like a dog who must have been in the building where the bed was.

We circled around so that we'd go back the way we had been earlier and, as we walked past a hedge, I sensed eyes glaring at me. I stuck my head through the branches and saw one of those creatures with short, pointed ears, but it looked so dangerous that I backed away. The person with the loop didn't notice, and we went on marching past, trying to catch up with the person who had the small dog. We caught up with them, but I kept glancing back at the creature who was still looking at me in that threatening way. I turned my head away so it would know that I meant no harm.

Out of danger, we turned a corner where I saw some more creatures, but thankfully, they were not the ones with the pointed ears; instead, they were more of the ones with the long ears. I pulled towards them, but the person with the loop grasped hold of the band around my neck and, reluctantly, I walked on behind the small dog with the teeth. We eventually reached some grass and I felt a desperate urge to go to the toilet, which I did. She then promptly got out a bag, gathered it up, and carried it along with her. They used to do that where I was before, and I'd become used to it, but

I still thought it was strange behaviour, because as far as I could see, if I hadn't wanted it there, then I wouldn't have put it there!

When we got back to the building, I was offered a piece of food. They also encouraged me to go up the steps. I really didn't want to go, but they made sounds that I liked, even though I didn't know what they were saying. Then they said "Ralph" over and over again, until eventually they put the loop onto the band on my neck and led me up the steps. I had been up there earlier when I was chasing the small dog, but I hadn't stayed up there and had just chased her back down again.

They led me into one of the rooms. I could smell the other dog I'd not seen, and they showed me to a soft place that didn't smell of the other dog, but the rest of the room did. It wasn't a threatening smell, like the scent of that creature with the pointed ears I had seen earlier, but it was a smell that puzzled me, as it smelt like a dog even though I couldn't see one.

One of them patted the soft place and put some more food in front of me. When I lay down they took off the loop and left me to eat the food, but I was too distracted to eat it. I was more interested in what they were doing. They left the room and then came back in smelling like flowers. Finally, they went and lay on the big, soft place that I had jumped on earlier when I had been chasing the small dog. I wondered where she was, but I had noticed another big, soft place down the steps. I figured she was in there with one of the other people. It suddenly became dark. I could hear gentle breathing sounds from the big bed, and thought they were maybe sleeping. I sighed and, very quietly, I ate the food they had given me. I then closed my eyes and went to sleep.

I was chasing the big friendly dog around the pen, and he was dancing around me. Then I saw the loop coming towards me, so I ran away. I turned, and the big dog had gone. Suddenly, the small dog was in front of me; her tail was erect, and she was showing her teeth. The gate opened, and then I was running, running, running. There was someone chasing me; I was cornered and couldn't get away from them. The pain across my muzzle hurt so much. Then came the taste of those creatures with the long ears. In the distance, I heard them calling, "Ralph...Ralph...Ralph!"

When I opened my eyes and saw the woman, I was confused. I licked my muzzle, but the taste had gone. I sniffed the air—there was a strong scent of the small dog with the teeth, and I could smell the dog I hadn't yet seen and the food they had given me before I had gone to sleep.

Then I remembered where I was and, while she gently stroked the side of my neck, I sank down into the soft warmth of the fluffy material beneath me, gave a long, deep sigh, and drifted into the deepest of sleeps.

CHAPTER 4

Us

We got Ralph home and it very quickly dawned on us that we had underestimated just how much support he was going to need. We had known when we met him that he was nervous, but we had never anticipated just how much whatever he had been through before had affected him. He was petrified of people and cowered away from us every time we tried to stroke his head. It became obvious that there was something in his past that had affected him terribly.

The scar across his muzzle was quite deep, and at first I found it extremely difficult even to look at that side of his face without having an intense feeling of sorrow that this large, and yet so delicate dog had at some point in his life endured something which resulted in his behaving in this way. We noticed he had other physical scars, one on his side and one on his leg; but above all else, we realised there was something in his psyche that made him believe that all people were to be feared.

Whether the behaviour and the scars were really linked we could only presume, but what we knew almost immediately was that, wherever and however this mistrust had originated, it had become our job to unravel it. We also knew there was not going to be an overnight transformation or miracle cure. The scar *could* have been caused by something as simple as barbed wire, but the injury combined with his behaviour suggested it was likely something much more sinister had happened in his past.

In addition to the scars I've already mentioned, Ralph at some point has had his front dewclaws removed. Strictly speaking, the front 'dewclaws' are not dewclaws at all (the term 'dewclaw' refers to the extra claw which sometimes is evident in a few dogs on the hind limb), and these claws we all think of as dewclaws are actually classed as the first digit of the dog's forelimb. They are therefore not truly covered by current UK legislation, which would allow the removal of 'dewclaws' by lay people before the puppy's eyes are open. The majority of these front digits (which are equivalent to our thumb and are actually used by a dog—if you watch them carefully when they are 'holding' something, you will see them using them) result in no damage to the dog at all. They therefore do not need to be removed unless they are proving to be troublesome, and then, as this would be when the dog is older, by a veterinary surgeon with the dog under an anaesthetic.

One of Ralph's claws appears to have been hacked off, leaving a small remnant of the claw behind. Whatever was done to the other side went completely wrong, and the claw has twisted around so that it now points forwards. In the words of a veterinary surgeon friend when she saw them, "They've certainly been butchered, haven't they?", as she shook her head and tried to make friends with this dog with the ears that make people smile. She handed him treats—treats that Ralph duly pushed out of her hand with his nose, and then picked up and ate from the floor.

We assumed that Ralph's dewclaws were cut off when he was a small puppy (and this would undoubtedly have happened without any anaesthetic) and, because of the type of dog he is, we suspected he was in the hands of people who had probably used him for hare coursing, which is illegal in the UK.

What we were told of his history was that he had been admitted to an animal rescue shelter as a stray and, having reached his 'time up', he was moved up to our local no-kill shelter. The staff in the first charity had been desperately phoning around other animal shelters to see whether anyone would be able to take him. Fortunately, more and more organisations are now doing this exchange of 'sticky' dogs (dogs that take a while to find a new family to love them) in an effort to find homes for as many dogs as possible. It may be that a dog who has been at an organisation for some time is simply being overlooked, or it could be that an organisation doesn't have the time to deal with a dog's particular requirements, and so they pass the dog on to someone else who has the space and time. Sometimes certain breeds rehome more easily in certain regions, so it makes sense for the dogs to be moved to where they will have the best chance of finding a home.

He ended up at our local rescue kennels, and we're so glad that he did. We're also glad that, in the current economic climate with more and more dogs being abandoned or put up for rehoming, they had the space to respond to the desperate plea of the other shelter. I only wish that we didn't live in a society in which these decisions were being made by so many rescue organisations all over the country every day. Some organisations reach a point of desperation when too many dogs enter their kennels. They lack the kennel space to care for them, so they resort to euthanasia. We live in a society in which there are too many dogs and not enough homes. While breeding of dogs goes on indiscriminately and people continue to make heaps of money from replenishing an already overflowing stock of dogs, the problem will never be resolved.

Once he was with us, in everything we did we had to consider Ralph's deep-rooted problems. The first step was resisting our natural urges to reach out and touch him on the head, which one of the most difficult interactions I've ever had with a dog, but that was better than Ralph having a constant fear response each time we tried to make friends with him. Frustratingly, we experienced several times each day when we'd forget, and out our hands would go to pat him on the head. He would immediately back off, recoiling like a spring, which just added to his fear and confusion, and our frustration. We became frustrated with ourselves and annoyed with the situation that had resulted in his ending up in such a state.

Frequently, there were times when he seemed to remember whatever had happened to him before, and he had what I can only describe as dog nightmares. He twitched and had involuntary movements that were not like other dogs' dreams when they 'chase bunnies' in their sleep. These sharp, jerking actions seemed to be much more deep-rooted than that. When he woke, he was disorientated, so we had to reassure him that everything was okay by talking soothingly to him and gently stroking the side of his neck. Even though he was wary, he let us stroke his head and talk to him when he was next to us on the sofa, but if we tried to approach him when he was standing, invariably he would run away and cower at the other side of the room. We learned very quickly not to put him under that pressure. We let our affection towards him be on his terms, and he seemed much more relaxed that way. Still, it wasn't easy because it went completely against our natural instincts not to approach him and fuss over him as you would with any other dog. Our friends had to learn quickly, too. Rather than approaching Ralph first, everyone talked to him and let him come closer to sniff them once he felt comfortable.

Like many nervous dogs, he was so obviously calmer and better with women than with men (perhaps it's the softer voice and gentler movements), but you could never guarantee who he would be good with. We therefore took each day at a time to let him progress at his own pace. We encouraged other people to use calming signals with him, as we did with him, too. Although they probably felt quite silly doing them, doing this helped him a great deal.

I have never in all my years of working with animals seen calming signals being used by a dog to the extent that they were evident in Ralph those first couple of months that we had him. His almost constant urge to placate us and to make us back off, was evident in a combination of actions that came one after another after another: lip smacking followed by stretching, followed by a deep yawn, and then lip licking and averting his eyes and turning his head to the side, followed by yet another deep yawn. Throughout this display, he was invariably searching for an escape route.

As I've already mentioned, while dogs use calming signals with each other, it can also be very effective to use them with a nervous dog. We did this to great effect in the early stages with Ralph. Rather than chasing him around the garden trying to get him back into the house when he was clearly too frightened to come in, we would go inside and call him. When he came to the door and stood there looking at us, stretching and yawning, we would simply avert our eyes and turn our backs away from him so he thought we were not interested in his presence and, more importantly, that we were no threat to him. Hey presto, he would then walk in behind us, all the time watching us. In doing this, we would take the pressure off him, and he would do what we had wanted him to do in the first place.

When Bob got home from work Ralph would be frightened because Bob is male, and we strongly suspected it was a male (or males) who could have mistreated him. To make things easy for Ralph, Bob would get down low so that he was lying on the ground, and then he would yawn and avert his eyes, lick his lips and stretch forward and, invariably, Ralph would move forward to sniff him. And we left it at that. To go further at that stage would have made Ralph take three steps back—or retreat to another part of the house away from everyone. We knew we simply had to take his development in tiny fairy steps, silently applauding his progress at each stage (but wanting to shout out with joy every time we felt as though we were reaching him).

Interestingly, early on he was better with our son, Anthony, than he was with Bob. Anthony is left-handed and therefore always approached Ralph with his left hand, whereas Bob, being right-handed, always approached him with his right hand. Ralph's scar is on the left side of his face, which suggests that it could have occurred because of someone attacking him with their right hand from the front. When Bob and I tried switching to left-handed approaches, we saw a subtle improvement—and any improvement was good. The only problem was that because it wasn't our 'natural' handedness, it was difficult to remember to approach him in this way.

So Ralph's calming signals came thick and fast with every single interaction he had with us being laden with them, and while he also did them with Luella, Mum's little teeth-baring dog, with her they were much less obvious. This was perhaps because with other dogs he realised he didn't have to be quite as deliberate in his communication, as dogs would pick up on much more subtle signals. It was also probably because he felt more comfortable with her—even though she was a bit of a tyrant when she was around him.

Although they stayed with us for only a few weeks, when Mum went home with Luella, we realised that for Ralph to have any chance of ever gaining trust in us, we would have to find him a permanent canine companion as soon as possible. This would preferably be one who didn't feel as though she constantly had to elevate herself above him and growl at him. However, even for all Luella's shows of bravery, having just joined the family herself, she too was just getting used to everyone, and the stay with us because of my brother being in hospital had been totally unexpected.

A lot of Luella's apparent aggression was really just a part of her establishing her own boundaries, and I'm sure it had a lot to do with the characteristics of the two breeds that are her genetic heritage! Whoever would have thought of doing something like crossing a Chihuahua with a Jack Russell terrier? Certainly not anyone who has spent any time working with these breeds, I think! If you take one type of dog who has every extreme terrier instinct and cross it with a breed that has the ingrained characteristics of years of defending the laps of their owners, then you end up with one very mixed up dog who doesn't really know what she is, or how she should behave. That said though, she is a great companion for a lady in her seventies, and she very much keeps Mum more active than she would be without her.

In addition to the excessive use of calming signals in Ralph, we had to contend with another part of his behaviour that had apparently been instilled in him from an early age: chasing rabbits or hares, and we had to encourage him to 'unlearn' that behaviour.

One glimpse of a rabbit (and they don't call them sight hounds for nothing), and he was leaping forward in an attempt to get loose to run after it and catch it. This occurred two or three times a day, a problem that we had to cope with right away. Having had lurchers before, we knew how very difficult it could be to stop the chase instinct when it had been used to the extent that it clearly was in a dog such as Ralph. Through rewarding him with treats and squeaky toys, we've had to make ourselves more interesting than the local rabbits! In their new forever homes, so often these dogs—who have been encouraged to chase and kill—are resigned to a much more sedentary life as pets and are only allowed to run off the lead in enclosed areas. This is a compromise those of us who love these dogs have come to accept.

As I have already mentioned, hare coursing is illegal in the UK. It takes place when a group of people get together in a hare's territory (or in an area in which they release a hare they have caught and caged from somewhere else) with their respective dogs. The dogs are let off their leads to chase the hare and, eventually, one of the dogs makes a kill. As if the cruelty to the hare isn't evidence enough that this practice should remain illegal, then the treatment of the dogs involved in the activity should be, as I have seen many which have made their way into rescue who are underweight, and in very poor condition. The dogs used are usually either greyhounds or lurchers—dogs with a strong chase instinct. A lurcher is a crossed greyhound and, historically, this was a greyhound crossed with a collie. You do see some lurchers around who clearly have this cross, but these days the term is used much more loosely in relation to any greyhound cross. Ralph's cross is probably saluki (somewhere along that line, at least) with a greyhound, but who knows?

These dogs are bred to create the fastest, fittest dogs, and those who don't make the grade are quite often cast aside. Eventually, if they are the lucky ones, they find their way to a rescue centre. You would hope that having come that far, they would then find a good home and live happily ever after, but again, this is not always the case. They have so often experienced months, or in some cases years, of poor handling and abuse resulting in an array of problems that need to be unravelled piece by piece and layer by layer. Only then will you have a contented family dog.

Unfortunately, having been trained to chase animals that invariably squeal when they are caught, these dogs often can't distinguish between the squeal of a hare and that of a cat, a pet rabbit or a small dog, which can sometimes create problems in a family situation. That aside, however, if you can overcome the majority of the issues they come to you with, and simply be aware of the rest and cope with them, then the rewards are incredible. They can be the most adaptable dogs and are usually happy travelling in the car, walking in the woods, exploring the hills, or simply lying on their backs on a comfortable sofa with their legs in the air. They can seem almost grateful eventually to find a home in which they are taken care of and, once they've been there a while, their behavioural issues become less apparent.

In Ralph's case, the main problems were his clear aversion to people, his desire to chase rabbits, and his fear of traffic and sudden, loud noises. We—having been terrified early on when his greyhound collar nearly came off while he was jumping around like a lunatic trying to chase rabbits—went out and purchased a harness for him. This would have the dual effect of making him safer around traffic

I have long since felt uneasy at the idea of leading a dog around by a collar and had intended on transferring him to a harness anyway, but this prompted us to do it sooner rather than later. Initially we had thought that too many changes at once would have been too much for him, and that had been the reason for the delay, but this had suddenly become a necessity. We immersed ourselves in learning about the harnesses that were available, as there were so many different types from which to choose. Some harnesses can hurt the dog, particularly on the chest behind the front legs. Eventually, thanks to the vast amount of patience of one of the store's assistants (I sometimes wonder how they cope with the demands of neurotic pet owners), we found a good design that clips either side of him just behind his front legs. It also has a piece across his back, preventing the gathering up of the harness, which in some other types can cause soreness and chafing of the skin.

While we realised that no harness could be completely infallible, for Ralph it gave us the additional confidence that he was as secure as he could be. His security enabled us to concentrate much more on his issues with people rather than his insatiable desire to chase rabbits.

He adapted very quickly to the harness, and it calmed him down remarkably whenever he saw any rabbits. Although he continued to do somersaults, he realised that it was more difficult to get away. He quickly, albeit reluctantly, resigned himself to the restraint. I think in some ways the harness gave him a sense of security, similar to the way 'storm jackets' give a very nervous dog a feeling of safety by applying pressure to his body, like being in the womb.

He adored Luella from the start, and Luella has quite definitely always been in charge whenever they've been together. She learned very quickly that, due to her size disadvantage, she needed to elevate herself above him whenever she could, and gradually he became much more comfortable when she was around. When she growled and snarled at him, he sometimes returned a small, playful *woof* (which quite remarkably at times sounded as though he was saying "Ralph" in a gruff voice) and play bowed. Other times, he tossed his head and walked away from her—expertly calming her while subconsciously calming the situation, in a way that only a dog like Ralph can.

He loved to play. Watching him play with other dogs warmed our hearts, as those were the times when he seemed to be really, truly happy, and with all that he'd been through you would have expected there might have been some sign of aggression. But there was nothing. We came to realise that Ralph didn't have an aggressive streak anywhere in his personality. All he wanted was to play with everyone and everything (especially if they were four-legged), so we knew that our greatest challenge was going to be his fear of people.

Summer

CHAPTER 5

Ralph

They stopped putting the loop around my neck. Instead, when they took me out I had this strange contraption attached over my head and then under my front legs, and it went *click-click* before they touched me on my head and ruffled my ears. Meanwhile, I turned my eyes away from them and sometimes yawned at them.

We had this routine going where we got up in the mornings and I followed them downstairs. They would say, "Ralph, Ralph," and I would go out and pee. When they called me back in again, I would watch them to try to figure out what they were doing in the place where they made the food. Then, when they turned their sides to the back door and worked away at making food, I would run through the door behind them. If I happened to jump on the mat as I ran behind them, this was a real bonus, as I would go sliding across the room. It was great fun!

I eventually got into the habit of running back into the building and waiting for them to get ready, and then they'd put the new loop around my neck, front legs and chest and clip it onto the top of my shoulders so we could go for a walk. Sometimes I would see the creatures with the pointy ears, but I'd keep away from them because they frightened me. Other times, I would see the animals that I knew tasted like my face did that time, and I'd try to chase them, but the thing they'd attached around my chest stopped me from leaping in the air like I could before.

After walking, we'd go back to the building, and after a rest, I'd have some food. Then I'd go out to the toilet, and they'd say, "Good boy, Ralph." We'd go through this routine later in the day and then again at night before we went to sleep. In between times, I'd play with my rope toys and rubber balls. I used to play with the small dog, but she'd gone away. I thought I knew where she'd gone though, because one day we went in the vehicle, and she was in another place with the person who used to be in the building where I live. I hoped I'd see the small dog again soon because she was fun to play with, and I used to chase her and pounce on her with my front paws. Mostly she didn't mind. Sometimes, though, she would show me those teeth. When that happened, I'd leave her alone for a while.

So the days mostly became the same, and sometimes there were many people in the building where I stayed—and sometimes only one, but most of the time someone was there to keep me company. I didn't like being on my own, and I think it had something to do with the sore part on my face, because when they came back I didn't know what they were going to do. I stayed where I was because I was so scared at what might happen to me if I peed on their big soft bed. I did this a couple of times, but they didn't shout at me or hurt me. Eventually I began to realise they were not going to hurt me when they came home, so I didn't pee anywhere. When I heard their vehicle pulling up outside, sometimes I ventured onto the stairs and sat and watched them walk through the front door. When they saw me, they called, "Ralph, Ralph," in a soft tone, so I went down the steps very cautiously, hoping no one would try to touch me. But they always let me walk past them and outside to the toilet. Once I'd been, they'd say, "Good boy, Ralph," and I would come back inside. Then they'd say "Good boy, Ralph," again, which would make me happy.

Sometimes we would all sit in the room with the comfortable seats, and they would pass around food that didn't smell much like the food that I ate, but they'd give me something to chew while they were eating. A box in the corner would make loud noises that I didn't understand, but they seemed to be happy, and sometimes I found a space on the soft seats next to them and they'd let me stay there. I would turn away from them so that my head was in the opposite direction. That way, they could stroke my back and my head and sometimes when they rubbed my shoulders and stroked my neck, I'd stretch out my legs and push up my toes because it made me relax.

Often we'd go in the vehicle to a place that smelt of lots of dogs and there were many trees, and we'd go for a walk. One day, when we all got in the vehicle and headed off, I thought that we were going to the trees, but it seemed to be taking a long time. Eventually we stopped at a place like the one with the dogs and the trees, and we stayed there a little while and went for a walk. Well, by then I was really crossing my legs and was desperate to go to the toilet. When I couldn't hold on any longer, I found a suitable place next to a bush and created the largest puddle. When we went back to the vehicle, I'd hoped we were going back to the building with the comfortable seats and the noisy box that they all watched, but we ended up somewhere else and they were carrying lots of bags.

They encouraged me to go up some stairs. I didn't want to, but I had no choice because of the loop that was around my chest. At the top of the steps was a building made out of something that smelt like trees and there were lots of real trees around it. Inside the building was a room with comfortable seats and another room that smelt like food. As I turned around, I saw one of them putting my soft bed next to the soft seats. Once they had removed the loop, I went over there, sat on it, and yawned at them. Then I sighed and licked my paws for a while.

When we'd rested and I'd eaten, we went off for a long walk in another place with both tall trees and short trees. We sat outside a place that smelt of food like the bread I used to scavenge from the birds when I didn't have anywhere to live. Nearby was an enclosure with a big puddle of water and some animals with wings were swimming in it. They looked at me with their funny noses and I wanted to run and chase them because they looked as though they'd be fun to chase, but I wasn't allowed.

Someone from inside the place that smelt of food came out and said something, and then we went and sat inside. But I was frightened because everything was so different. Some people tried to touch me on the head, but the one holding my loop stroked me on the side of my neck. I couldn't stop shaking. Finally, the other people backed off. The people I live with ate some food and passed some bits of what they were eating down to me where I lay on the floor. It tasted okay, but I preferred the food I had had earlier. I spat it on the floor and poked it around with my nose.

It was nighttime when we went outside again, and the winged animals we had seen on the water earlier were resting. When I tried to pull towards them, they stood up and squealed at me. The person with the loop called me away from them, so off we went for a walk through the trees. When I'd been to the toilet and they'd said, "Good boy, Ralph," they picked up what I had done on the ground in one of those small bags. We went back to the place where we had left my soft bed. At bedtime, they moved my soft bed into the other room and we all went to sleep. When I woke the next morning, I wondered where I was, but they put the loop on me and we headed to the trees again. My heart skipped a beat because I saw the winged creatures with the funny noses again and a dog who looked just like the big, black dog. She wagged her tail at me, but she had a loop around her neck and I had one around my chest, so it was difficult to play.

Later on, we went for a ride in the vehicle. After a short time, we ended up at a place where the air smelt strange. I sniffed through the open window but couldn't quite make out what was different. When we stopped and I jumped out, the smell got much stronger. We walked for a while and there were stones that seemed to move beneath my feet. Then my chest started pounding when I saw a giant, monstrous figure not very far away. It was huge and moving, and looking at it made me feel very weird. They made me walk closer to it, but I jumped away and tried to pull back. "Ralph," they kept on saying. When I looked up at them, they showed me their teeth like the little dog, and I was scared. As we got closer, they held the loop tighter. It smelt even stronger the closer we got. As we got right up to the creature's edge, another dog ran into its mouth and then immediately came running back out again. What on earth was he doing? I looked back up at the people on the end of the loop; they were still looking back at me—showing me their teeth and saying, "Ralph!"

When we reached the large moving creature, I felt very silly, because it was only water. It kept moving away and then back towards me again; splashing in front of me as it crept towards my feet. The people with the loop were making happy noises and screeching as it got closer to them, too, and they seemed to be excited, so I wasn't frightened. We walked along the edge of the water. I was a little thirsty, so I lapped some of it. Then I spat it out; it didn't taste as good as the puddles. Right then, the one holding the loop started to run next to the water, so I had no choice but to run, too. It was good fun—except that he couldn't quite keep up with me, so I had to slow down my pace a little.

We spent ages trying to catch the moving water—but we never did.

After a long walk we turned and walked back to the vehicle and, on the way, I saw something strange high up in the sky, fluttering in the wind. I didn't know what it was, so I looked at the people with the loop to see if they were watching it. They *were* watching it *and* their mouths were open wide, which I thought was strange. I don't think they knew what it was either.

Back at the vehicle, they opened the back and I jumped in. They poured some water in a bowl, I tried some, and although it tasted better than the big water, it still wasn't as good as a puddle, so I just took a few laps and then turned away from it. As the vehicle moved along, I looked behind me to make sure neither the big watery monster nor the strange object from the sky was following me. Thankfully they weren't.

We stopped at a place where they took me along some paths lined with stones, flowers and long grass. We took our time walking there. A gentle breeze lifted my ears, and they began flapping gently. I lifted my nose to sniff the air and it was lovely. Eventually they took me back to the vehicle and we made our way back to the place where my soft bed was. I was so tired that I slept and they had to wake me up for my food. That night was the same as the previous day when before bedtime we had gone for a nice walk under the trees. Again, I could smell the friendly dog who looked like the big black dog, but she wasn't there.

We visited another place that had more moving water monsters, only this time there was a strange soil beneath my feet; it was getting stuck between my toes as I kept sinking into its fine grains. The smell was extremely strong again, and the water was moving the same as before, but this time I tried hard to be brave and not to jump away from it, but it was still very frightening, so I did. Later, when we walked along the water's edge, the coldness of the water caught my toes. But it didn't hurt, so I didn't jump away. The person with the loop walked in deeper, but I just stayed at the edge because I didn't want to get my feet too wet.

Next we went in our vehicle to a place where there was water falling. It was noisy and I didn't like that. I felt happier when we went back and went for a walk through some trees instead. Some people I didn't recognise came over to us. I think they were talking about me because they were watching me all the time. I backed away from them so they would stop trying to touch me. Then I felt better. When those people went away, someone else came over, but she didn't stay as long. That night, back where my soft bed was, the box in the corner of the room made some strange sounds while everyone, including me, sat around eating. Finally, we went to sleep.

The following day, we went on a long, long journey. I was tired of seeing all the vehicles and the trees and houses going by, but eventually we arrived at the building we'd left from before the other long journey—I was home.

They put my soft bed back inside and I followed them. Then I went to look for the small dog with the teeth.

But she wasn't there.

CHAPTER 6

Us

When we started the long road in our attempts to communicate with Ralph, more so than with any other dog we'd ever had, I became aware of the fact that he was a dog and I was a person. We are not the same species as our dogs, and although we like to think that they understand us (and they do pick up on our body signals extremely well, even if some of them are confusing, like the smile of a human versus the raised lips of dogs like Luella), their concept of our verbal language is very limited. Understanding that these difficulties exist can help us as owners to appreciate that we have to show our dogs how to do something, or show them what we want from them, in a very specific way in order to prevent any confusion.

From early on in our relationship with Ralph, we used calming signals with him as often as possible, which seemed to help him to accept that we were not a threat. He urinated on our bed a few times, and each time we had to buy a new duvet. We realised that the urination was happening just as we arrived home (it was always still fresh and warm!), and it registered with us that he was probably doing it out of fear when he heard us pull up on the drive. We resolved it by not going to find him to greet him when we got home, as he was clearly terrified of what might happen when we approached him. Instead, we called him to us or just let him come to us in his own time. Very soon after doing this, when we arrived home he'd be sitting on the stairs, watching through the stair window as he waited for us—and there was no wet bed!

Just five weeks after getting him and settling him into life with us as much as we possibly could, we upset his whole routine by taking this poor, mixed up hound on holiday with us to the Highlands. As part of this excursion, we went on a hundred-mile diversion to collect Anthony's girlfriend. Being a busy Friday (reminding us why we don't ever normally travel on a Friday), the whole journey took nearly nine hours. By the time we all got there, our yawns were real ones and not the ones that we, as mere humans, were feigning to pacify Ralph.

In the desperate hope that we would have one more holiday with Oskar, several months before he died we had booked the holiday for four people plus one dog. We had known that he was fading fast but had hoped that he would have been with us a little longer. In some ways, I guess we were trying to make a deal with fate and, subconsciously, were hoping we'd be able to have just one more holiday that would allow us to create fresh memories of this old gentleman. Unfortunately, it wasn't to be. As part of my grief after losing him, there was this desperate urge for us to find another dog to take on holiday. In my mind was the simplistic practical aspect of the situation: we had paid for a dog to go, so we may as well take one. Another part of me knew the holiday would have been empty without a dog. Therefore, even though we'd only had Ralph for just over four weeks by the time we were packing the car roof box, there he was, going on his first family holiday.

To observe a dog who was quite clearly seeing the sea for the first time was such a joy, and that day on the coastline of the beautiful Scottish Highlands, we witnessed this dog's metamorphosis from a frightened, nervous creature into a brave hound dog running around the beach, dragging Bob around on the end of a lead. He seemed to love the scent of the ocean and the combination of sand, seaweed, and pebbles beneath his toes and, just for a short while, he seemed to have lost all his fears. We felt triumphant when we finally managed to get him to dip his toes in the water's edge.

On the campsite where we were staying in a log cabin, in spite of all the changes he'd experienced over the previous weeks, he coped extremely well and seemed to enjoy his walks through the forest to the lake. At the entrance to the forest was a small restaurant. The first night we stayed on the site there was no one else around, so, rather than eat outside where it was starting to get a little chilly (which we should have done because we had a dog with us), the restaurant staff allowed us to sneak Ralph inside where he lay on the carpet next to our table.

One of the women who worked behind the bar came over to speak to him, and he immediately cowered into the corner. Then, of course, we found ourselves relating his whole life history to her, as much as we knew of it anyway, to let her know that it wasn't us who had caused the fear response that is so evident in him. Those first few months that we had him, we told the story repeatedly. Each time we had to explain that he had been transferred from a rescue shelter where he'd reached his 'time up', to one near to where we live, and that, no, we didn't know what had happened to his face. At times, it almost made us feel defensive, and I began to wonder whether people believed us. This made me despise the people even more who had done what they did to Ralph to make him the way he had become.

We visited a waterfall—Shin Falls—where, interestingly, I fell down some steps and hurt my shin, but that's another story. While there, we chatted with several people, most memorably a man and his father who came over to speak to us because they, too, had a lurcher. Their lurcher had been very nervous when they had first taken him to live with them, but over the years, he had become quite confident. It was good to hear about a dog who had recovered from similar nervous tendencies and it gave us hope for Ralph's future.

Later, while I was browsing in the gift shop and Bob and Ralph were waiting very patiently outside, a woman came over to speak to Bob. She'd noticed Ralph's ears and wanted to know why they were like that and not like they *should* have been. Gosh, people are funny, aren't they? Ralph's ears are like that because they're Ralph's ears, and there's absolutely nothing wrong with them. He never declared that he was a greyhound. Bob told her that his ears are like that because he's a rescue dog, and rescue dogs don't come to order and that we think he's gorgeous. Browbeaten, the woman went away.

Dogs attract people to come and talk to you and, where people would normally walk past you without making eye contact, they greet you and sometimes stop to chat. This is far more evident when you have a relatively rare breed. Our friends have deerhounds, and people stop all the time to talk to them and their dogs. In Ralph's case, although he's not a rare breed, he has an unusual appearance, and it's certainly his almond-shaped eyes and floppy ears that people seem drawn to. He also has a trotting gait that looks quite peculiar when he's walking (or trotting) along, and when he sees another dog, he falls down into a play bow and jumps around like an absolute lunatic. He did this when we met the dog in the forest on holiday; she was a gorgeous golden retriever and really just a big puppy. When Ralph saw her, he just wanted to play. We were told that Ralph was eighteen months old when we got him, but the more we got to know him, the more I began to believe that when we brought him into our family, he couldn't have been much more than a year old. On the other hand, perhaps he missed out on a normal puppyhood, and this was him experiencing playfulness for the first time?

Whenever he saw another dog and behaved so playfully, it was difficult for people to believe that he was the same dog who would cower away from them if they tried to touch him. As time has gone on, we have become better at warning people that it's better not to touch him, as we don't want him to be stressed. He seems far more relaxed because of this, and mostly I think it's because we're doing things his way and at his pace.

Travelling to the Highlands over nine hours was difficult enough for the human residents in the car—in fact, it made Anthony and his girlfriend virtually moribund for the time we were away. For a dog who had been in the family for only a few weeks, however, and an extremely nervous dog at that, it must have been quite an ordeal! We stopped on the way beside the (Bonnie, Bonnie, Banks of) Loch Lomond and walked Ralph through the trees down a short forest path, patiently willing him to go to the toilet so we could make our way onto the next leg of our journey. We walked and we walked, trying to figure out what it is about dogs that when you are desperate to get moving, they seem to sense this, and they develop an element of stubbornness that manifests itself as a reluctance to go to the toilet.

We went around the forest walk twice, as we were convinced he needed to go, but that he must have been distracted by strange scents and different sounds. In the end, as we made our way back to the car for the second time, he practically exploded as urine gushed out of him. You could see the look of relief finally passing across his face.

Desperate for him to have a drink, we poured some water in a bowl for him, but he turned his head away from it. Probably less than half of the dogs we've ever had have been happy to drink from a bowl with water we've carried especially for them. You think they must be so desperate for water, but so often there's this same reaction, and they don't drink until they get to their destination when they can have fresh water from the tap or, preferably, a dirty puddle. After offering Ralph some water several times, we gave up and poured the water onto the ground, before heading off to our holiday home.

This is a prime example of the fact that we can talk to our dogs until we're blue in the face about how it's going to be another two and a half hours until we get to where we're going or to the next possible rest stop, but no, they don't understand. Dogs don't seem to have any concept of the future in that context, just the here and now. It's almost as though they're saying, "If it doesn't smell like the water at home, then I'm NOT going to drink it. I'll wait until I find something that smells 'just right'!"

We took him to the site of the Battle of Culloden. After a few initial scares when we were getting him out of the car, he seemed at ease and appeared to enjoy walking along the cultivated paths and stopping with us every now and then as we read the information boards and gravestones in memory of all those who fell in the mid-1700s. There was a warm summer breeze, and I felt that Ralph was truly relaxed as he trotted along beside us. He had found the beaches interesting, but as everything had been so new there for him, his curiosity had seemed to distract him, whereas at Culloden he was surrounded by long grass and the beautiful scents emanating from the meadow flowers. I think that for the first time, possibly in his whole life, he was in some kind of doggie heaven. His face had relaxed and he turned his head in the direction of the breeze; catching the scent of the fresh, clean air from the hills.

Back at the camp, he developed a fancy for a Muscovy duck that was kept on a pond among some other ducks and geese. Whether Ralph liked it because he wanted to chase it and eat it, or whether he genuinely wanted to play with it, we weren't sure. Fortunately for the bird, however, it was behind a tall chain-link fence, and any communication between the two of them was done through the gaps between the wires. The bird wasn't exactly chuffed each time it saw Ralph, but Ralph was overjoyed, jumping around in circles to get its attention, which a few times it wasn't keen on giving. When it saw him approaching, the bird simply curled its neck around and placed its head underneath its wings—a seemingly deliberate reproach from one species to another.

Domesticated dogs have trouble enough in communicating with animals of their own species, let alone communicating with two entirely different species. I am talking, of course, of the enforced companionship we impose upon them that results in their having to spend their lives with us humans and, in many households, that other four-legged friend—THE CAT.

A large proportion of our communication, either intra-species or inter-species, is through body language, and dogs are fantastic observers of the finest of signals when communicating with each other. They are able to interpret these signals and then act accordingly with the fastest of responses. When they apply these same observation skills to humans and cats, they don't have to look very far to notice really obvious body language that indicates our thoughts and intentions. The only problem is (and it can be a huge problem in some circumstances), the signals we humans and cats use don't always match up with the ones used by dogs, and this inevitably leads to confusion. For instance, and very simply, in cats a waving tail will often indicate that the cat is getting cross with someone or something, and a human smiling and showing his or her teeth usually means they are happy! Compare these two signals to what they mean in a dog, and you get the picture. With many dogs, it doesn't seem to matter so much, as they've often had time since they were tiny pups to get used to normal behaviour in people and other creatures. If you have a dog like Ralph who is poorly socialised, however, then you have to rethink your behaviour completely, and the actions that normally come naturally to you have to be modified. Essentially, that's what we had to do with Ralph. We knew that our behaviour changes wouldn't need to be permanent, though—just long enough for us to earn his trust.

After the holiday, I felt the trust was coming; we had managed to get through what could have been an extremely stressful holiday, and we'd become even more drawn to his sweet ways. We really enjoyed our time in the Highlands and all the places we had taken Ralph. I felt that he was becoming much more confident. When we got back home, we continued with the huge task of trying to build on this confidence he had gained. In the back of our minds, we knew we'd only be at work for two more weeks before our long summer break, which was when we planned to find him a canine companion. We hadn't forgotten our promise to the staff at the rescue kennels that we would find Ralph a friend as soon as possible.

Life has a way of waiting for you to relax when you've been really focused on something you're concerned about, and just when you let your guard down a little, just when you think things are progressing well, you're presented with a problem—something that requires you to re-evaluate everything and consider making quite drastic changes to your life. Something that Ralph did the week after we returned from our holiday made us do just that.

CHAPTER 7

Ralph

They put my loop around my chest so I could go out for a walk. I quite liked walks because I loved to be able to go out to see the other dogs. I hadn't seen the little dog with the teeth for a while, or the person who had been there when I arrived, although I could sometimes smell the little dog on the people who live in the building with me, and who put the loop over my head and around my chest. Sometimes when we went out I heard loud noises from huge vehicles, but we couldn't go anywhere from the building we lived in without walking past them. I was always glad when we got to the piece of ground away from the vehicles, and then we could go for a long walk without going near them. Unfortunately, though, we always had to come back that way to get to our home.

One day we walked past the vehicles, which were loud and fast, but I held my breath until we got past them. The people kept on saying "Ralph" and some other words I didn't understand, so I just tugged on the band that was around my chest to get onto the ground around the corner. Then it was okay, so I relaxed a little. I began looking for the creatures with the long ears who stayed still whenever they saw me coming, and then when we got closer to them they'd run. They were very fast, but still I couldn't reach them because I had the band around my chest holding me back. I was sure I would be faster than they would be...if only I was loose.

We walked between the trees, and I saw the dog with the long ears who I wanted to play with. I also saw the big dog who looked like the big black dog, only he was a shade of yellow. I noticed that he didn't have a loop on, but he stayed near to the person who was with him. I wouldn't do that if I didn't have my loop on! How could he resist chasing the creatures with the big ears or coming over to play with me? He trotted past me and hardly looked in my direction, which made me think that he was actually quite rude.

At the top of the part of the walk with the trees, we headed back home. I trotted along beside them and, every now and then, pulled away a little from the vehicles. The people kept on making noises that sometimes sounded like "Ralph." Everything was okay, but then I saw some people coming up towards us, and there was nowhere for us to go because the vehicles were in the way. The people moved out of the way, but I felt trapped as we walked past them. They were looking down at me and showing me their teeth, but the vehicles were coming so I edged away from them. But then there was a pain in my foot, and I couldn't cope. The one with the loop was tugging back on the band around my chest. I backed away and panicked, but there were people in front of me, and vehicles behind me, and I didn't know where to go. I wanted to go with the one who was holding my loop. Her voice got louder and louder as she called me, "Ralph! Ralph!" I was getting more and more scared. A vehicle screeched and stopped right behind me, but people were still in front of me, so I pulled back and ducked my head down low.

I felt the band come over my head.

I was free.

I ran and I ran, away, away, away from the vehicles and back to our house, but the entry at the front was closed. I stopped because they were calling me and I didn't know what to do, but then I chose instead to go to the place where the animals were with the big ears—away, away from the vehicles and away from the people. The ones with the loop were still calling, and I could hear them faintly in the distance, but I couldn't go to them because that was where the vehicles were—and the pain in my foot.

I continued to run as fast as I could. In front of me, a vehicle had stopped, but I managed to get past it. Confused, I kept running. Even though I could still hear them calling I wanted to get to where it was quiet. I could hear something pounding in my chest. It was the same sound I heard when I had my ear next to another dog. This was much, much louder, though. I was hot, and my tongue was hanging out of my mouth.

I had reached the place where the creatures with the ears usually were, but they weren't there, so I ran on through the trees. Someone was coming down the hill in my direction, and she was on one of those vehicles people sit on and move their legs. She slowed down to get out of my way, and I kept on running. I recognised where I was, but it was not where I wanted to be. I ran on, but I had gone the wrong way because when I got to the top, there were more of those loud vehicles. I didn't know which way to go, so I just picked what I thought might be the right way and then turned into a place where there were many buildings. I could smell the creatures with the long ears. I thought I knew where I was, but I was exhausted. When I reached some soft ground and found a huge plant to stop underneath out of the sun, I stopped to rest. I could hardly breathe.

As I sat there with my mouth gaping open and my tongue hanging down, I could hear something that made my chest tighten with fear. I turned slowly and saw him standing there. He was reaching out to me so I pulled back. I remembered what had happened before. My chest was bursting and my foot was throbbing. I recalled the pain across my face, though I couldn't quite remember how it happened. He reached closer to me. I cowered back into the leaves.

As he backed away from me, I backed even further away from him, retreating into the coolness of the plant. He was making sounds and they didn't make any sense to me. His eyes were looking into mine, but I looked away and yawned. I scanned the area to find somewhere that I could run and, looking past him, I saw another person coming towards us. He looked like the one who ruffled my ears a lot, but I wasn't sure. I looked the other way to see whether there was somewhere for me to go, but I couldn't escape. I had been right; the tall one was suddenly in front of me, reaching out to touch me. He smelt of the food they had eaten earlier—the type of food that I am not allowed to have.

The female who was often with him was standing right behind him. She made noises and crouched down on the ground not far away from me. I didn't know whether to go to her or whether to turn and try to get past them. She reached out to touch my face. She smelt like the fruit in the room where I eat my food. Then she reached forward and touched my neck. When I froze, she retreated. Then I saw another man I recognised coming over to me; he had a loop with him.

I panicked when he got closer. I remembered that there had been a pain in my foot and across my face, but I couldn't remember why. I knew I had to run, so I escaped past them all. They followed me, so I ran away from them. A vehicle stopped in front of me, so I stopped, too, but then I didn't know where to go. I saw the grass and the long-eared creatures running away, and I wanted to chase them, but they reached the bushes before I could catch them. The people were still following me so I headed for the bushes where the long-eared creatures had been. They were gone. When I turned around, I saw that I was surrounded. Someone with two other small dogs on loops was standing nearby, so I went over to see them, constantly watching the ones who were trying to catch me. The dogs were friendly, and they stayed a while. Even though I was temporarily distracted, those who were trying to put the loop over my head kept on trying to catch me. I was scared.

The small dogs were taken away on their loops. I really wanted to go with them, but then I saw someone else coming over to me who looked familiar. She was with another person who had a dog who was nearly the same size as me, but not quite. One of them had a loop. She smelt of the big, black dog who used to let me reach out and touch him with my paws when he was sleeping. I was confused and couldn't understand why she smelt like him. She held out a piece of food, which I managed to knock out of her hand. I picked it up and ate it. Then she gave me another one, and I did the same thing again. The other dog got a piece, too, so I moved my tail from between my legs as I stood up to sniff her. As I leaned forward, the one with the treats put a loop around my neck.

They had caught me, but strangely, I felt very secure.

We sat on the soft ground. They gave me and the other dog more pieces of food and made confusing sounds in my direction. I thought that they were good sounds. Then I remembered that when I had been walking past the vehicles, I had been with her, the one who gives me food in my bowl and who lets me snuggle beside her when she's watching the box in the corner that makes lots of strange, loud noises. I remembered there had been a pain in my foot and a lot of loud vehicles, and I could hear her saying, "Ralph! Ralph!" I was running, but I couldn't see her. All I wanted was to go back to her and that place where we all sleep.

Everybody surrounded me. And then I saw someone walking towards us. I shrank away a little, but then I realised that it was her. I wanted to pull to get to her, but she was coming towards us anyway. She came right up to me, held my neck, and put her head down so that her face was close to my head. She made soft, squeaking sounds by my ear. She was trembling. The top of my head was getting wet but I didn't know why. There was certainly no water coming from the sky. I would have known if it had been because I hated it when I got wet.

Even though it was getting wet on top of my head, I felt secure again. The one with the food gave me some more. I thought I might have had more than the other dog because she showed me her teeth like the little dog often did. An angry sound even came from her throat. I didn't know for sure whether it was because of me.

We sat for a while longer. The heat from the sky was changing, and I thought it was getting cooler. They put the extra loop around my chest, and then we headed off home. Not long after we got there, I had my food and, feeling quite exhausted, I headed for my soft bed where I rested my head on my front paws. I looked across to where she was sitting. She was staring at me, her eyes were shining and she was wiping her face with a soft piece of paper. When she saw me looking at her, she came over and sat beside me; she hugged me tight like before. She put her face on top of my head and made that squeaking sound again.

Confused because my head was getting wet again, I let out a deep sigh, closed my eyes, and went to sleep.

CHAPTER 8

Us

I thought I had lost him; I really did.

I thought his confidence had been improving. Just the week before, we had taken him almost three hundred miles away on holiday, for heaven's sake! We had walked him in thick forests, taken him to see a waterfall, chatted to people outside gift shops, taken him to the seaside and run across the beach with him. Yet, there we were, back on home territory and traipsing the streets, frantically trying to find him.

We had been on our way home from his evening walk and were walking towards the traffic about fifty yards from our house. It was rush hour and we were on the very narrow footpath along our street when I spotted three women heading in our direction. We would normally have stepped into a driveway to let anyone walking in the opposite direction pass us safely but, in this case, they stepped into a driveway to allow us to pass them, which meant we were on the path's edge right next to the traffic. I have relived that moment so many times and wished that I had stepped into the previous drive and let them go on, but I didn't. You can't go back and change that one momentary decision that seems to be fairly innocuous at the time, but which inadvertently sets off a chain reaction of events.

As we walked past the three women, Ralph stepped towards me, and I accidentally trod on his toe. He squealed and, Ralph being Ralph and not wanting to step back towards the women, he pulled back and tossed his whole body into the road. We have often thought of the footpath as being dangerous because it is so narrow that you have to walk very close to the traffic. I imagine that in his panic he saw the momentary gap in the traffic and jumped for it. Unfortunately, another car was coming, but luckily for us, the driver saw him and managed to do an emergency stop. Meanwhile, Ralph was pulling back on his harness, and while I tried to get him back onto the pavement, he slipped it and shot off down the road.

When all this drama happened we were just a few houses away from our house, and as we screeched his name in a desperate attempt to get him to come back, he reached our drive and headed over to the front door. For one moment, I thought he was safe, and I was so relieved that some kind of common sense had prevailed. He had gone straight home, but unfortunately, on realising the front door was closed, he did an immediate U-turn. Just as Bob reached the driveway, and with me a few paces behind, Ralph came out of the drive and disappeared down the road, amid the now very congested traffic. He was running in a blind panic. We shouted after him, desperately trying to penetrate the fear that had engulfed him.

My mouth was dry and my head spinning as I saw his tail disappear into the thick of the traffic. All I could think was that I had lost him, and that I would never see him again. I thought he would end up causing an accident and that these few short weeks were all that we would ever have with him. If he didn't end up involved in an accident, I felt sick with the mental image of his being found by someone who would treat him badly and that we would never know what had become of him.

I could hardly speak due to the increasing dryness in my throat, and as Bob raced off after him, I rushed into the house and shouted to Anthony and his girlfriend to come out and help us look for him. While they got their shoes on, I rushed out of the front door and down the road, desperately trying to anticipate which way he had gone, and which way Bob might have gone after him. I thought that if I went a different way, it would be easier to corner him and catch him. All this was to no avail. As I wandered the streets, I saw no sign of either of them and only hoped that, wherever they were, they were together. My limbs would eventually not allow me to run anymore, and my chest was sore from a combination of running and the surge of adrenaline charging through my body. I stopped for a minute and tried to gather my thoughts and catch my breath.

I realised that I needed to let as many people as possible know he was missing. Hence, with the image of my poor, terrified dog at the forefront of my mind and with tears in my eyes, I started knocking on the doors of all the people who I knew to be regular dog walkers in the hope that they would look out for him when they were out with their own dogs. I also spoke to everyone I passed, asking them if they would look out for my dog and gave them all my address in case they were to come across him. I explained they would be very unlikely to be able to catch him due to his extreme nervousness, and just to let us know if they caught sight of him.

My one saving grace through all of this—my one glimmer of hope, and what I told myself over and over again, was that he was identichipped. Because he had slipped his harness, he also still had his collar and identity tag on. At least that was something. Embroiled in every positive thought I had, however, were a hundred negative ones. Simultaneously I tried to tell myself that it was going to be okay and that we would soon have him back home with us, but lurking in the back of my mind was the recurring thought that he might have headed down to the bypass, which was only about a mile from our house.

Increasingly desperate, completely exhausted, and having not seen Bob, Anthony, or his girlfriend for what seemed like ages, I continued knocking on people's doors. Eventually, after knocking on the door of one dog owner, I decided to go next door to her neighbour who was the mother of Liz, one of the members of staff from the local rescue kennels where we had found Ralph.

At that time, Liz was also the housemate of one of my work colleagues, and between them, they had four rescue dogs. They both live and breathe anything to do with animals and, unknown to me as I disappeared back up the road searching frantically for a sign of Ralph, Liz's mother immediately texted her. On hearing of Ralph's plight, Liz and Jennie bundled themselves and Jennie's dog Trixie into one of their cars and headed for the streets to join in the search for him.

My heart pounded in my chest as each step I took I grew more and more desperate to find him. The thought of never seeing him again, of his ending up how he had been before—those were the images that pounded through my mind. All I wanted was to save him and keep him safe from harm. My throat and mouth were parched, so I made my way back to the house for a drink. I also had an inkling that he might have made his way back there, and that he might be waiting for me by the door when I returned. My heart sank when I saw there was no sign of him. When I pushed the handle down on the front door, I realised it was locked. Anthony had locked it when they'd gone off to join in the search. By then, desperate for water, I knocked on my neighbour's front door. Having drunk a glass of water, I returned to wait outside my front door—just in case he came back home.

We live on a main road and people were making their way back home from work on bicycles, in cars, and on foot. I stopped everyone who passed on foot and asked whether they had seen him—all to no avail. With each negative reply, my chest got tighter and my heart felt heavier, until the feelings of intense thirst returned. I made my way to some other neighbours to ask for some water to quench my thirst and to use their phone.

Unlike cats, dogs are considered as being property in the UK and therefore, when you lose one, you must contact the police. There is also the chance, property aside, that your dog might cause an accident. With this in mind, I rang the local police to let them know what had happened. The person who answered could not have been more helpful, and was clearly distressed as I blurted out my story. All the time I wondered just how much sense I was making. I phoned our veterinary practice to let them know so they, too, could look out for him. All the local surgeries were by then on the verge of closing for the evening and, still imagining I wouldn't ever see Ralph again, I told myself that the first thing I'd do the next day would be to phone every veterinary clinic in the area. With each minute that passed, I became increasingly desperate to find this mixed-up dog who had stolen my heart.

How long does it take for an animal to take your heart in that way? How long for you to realise they've become a part of you? That there's a need deep inside you to nurture and protect them? How long? Probably just a few minutes, I think, because there is something inside each of us as a species, some desire to nurture, that can be satisfied by taking care of an animal. Probably, too, because we have designed our dogs to look like babies with big, wide eyes and cute faces, and they have a sense of vulnerability, our love for them can be virtually instantaneous. And so, even though by that time Ralph had only been in our lives for six or seven weeks, he was already a part of our family, and we loved him.

I waited outside with my neighbours, Carla and Steven, wondering what to do next. Should I go off looking for him? Alternatively, should I stay put in case he found his way home? Carla suggested that I phone Bob. Sometimes the solutions to our problems are the simplest ones and being caught up in my fears about where Ralph was and what was happening to him, I had forgotten that, by this time, Bob may have found him.

I got hold of Bob on Carla's phone. He had, indeed, been trying to contact me, but absolutely typically for me, my mobile was ringing to itself in the house in the pocket of my work jacket, which was slung over the banister just where I'd thrown it when I had returned from work.

They had found Ralph, and they wanted me to come quickly because he wouldn't let anyone get near him.

Like jelly, my exhausted legs carried me the ten-minute walk to the location Bob had indicated. Carla went in the opposite direction, just in case in the meantime Ralph became frightened and decided to bolt again. As I approached the place where I thought they were waiting, a feeling of dread filled the pit of my abdomen as I saw Carla coming in my direction. Where were they? We had been around in a loop, so one of us should have come across them. When she was about fifty yards away from me, she said something that sounded like she hadn't seen them. She repeated what she had said as we got closer to each other, but I still couldn't make it out and I kept on walking towards her. Finally, she turned and pointed behind her and said, "It's okay! They've got him!"

And there he was—my dear, sweet, frightened dog.

As I took each step towards them, all I could focus on was him watching me, and then his ears pricked forward as he recognised me. I felt my whole face dissolve into a flood of tears. They had eventually managed to get him on a lead. Through the skillful teamwork of Liz and Jennie, helped by the presence of Jennie's dog Trixie and a supply of dog treats, they had managed to loop a slip lead over his head and around his neck so that he was well and truly caught. I flopped down on the grass beside him and pulled him close to me. I needed to know for sure that he was okay and to feel the warmth of his soft fur next to my face.

Only those who have loved a dog will understand the relief I felt, and how all the emotions of the previous hour disappeared—yes, just an hour, even though it felt like that hour had spanned a whole day. My emotions were replaced by what would appear on the opposite side of an emotional spectrum: sadness became elation and turbulence became calmness.

Ralph's heart was still pounding and, very gingerly, he accepted treats from Liz: tools of the trade that were stored in her fleece pocket. At one point, Trixie was quite offended as she clearly thought that Ralph was being offered more treats than she was; she quite rightly deserved all the treats she could muster for the part she had played in capturing Ralph. He cowered away a little as his newly found friend snapped at him for having an extra treat, but his love of other dogs was not going to be marred by a little bit of canine envy. After all, he was already getting used to the wrath of Luella!

With him on the slip lead, we put his harness back on him and used it in combination with the lead to encourage him back home. He was clearly still quite wary, but we had him back. Once inside the house, we all collapsed with sheer exhaustion. Bob runs to keep fit, and the rush of adrenaline had made him run faster and further than he normally would at a sprint. He was shattered, but we all had work to do and set about planning how we were ever going to thank the many people who had helped us to track him down and catch him. In the end, we bought small gifts and distributed them to these wonderful people. Many were strangers who had rallied round to help us in pursuit of this crazy, mixed-up dog; a dog who had entered our lives bearing such a tortured soul.

We realised more than ever we needed to fulfill the promise we had made to the staff at the rescue shelter (and ourselves)—to find Ralph a friend. The time was drawing nearer to the day when we would be able to bring another dog home. Without delay, we set out to find a suitable dog, quite tentatively at first, however, because the dog we adopted would need to complement Ralph's personality. We had to be very careful in our choice: another nervous dog would have been an absolute mistake, because it was likely they would have fed off each other's nervousness; an over-exuberant dog would have overshadowed him, and he would have been more apt just to exist inside his shell, while the other dog wallowed in the attention.

Once again, we brought up the Internet sites for all the major dog charities locally and within a hundred-mile radius of our home.

And there she was, in a photograph displayed on the rehoming web page for our local greyhound rescue charity—this strange looking black and white greyhound, who was pictured nose to nose with a donkey.

Her name was Peggy.

CHAPTER 9

Ralph

The little dog with the teeth had vanished, along with the lady who was often with her—the one who smelt of packets of strong-smelling white sweets. These sweets also smelt like the green plant that grows in a pot at the back of the building where we live. I missed the small dog very much. Then, one day, they put me back into the vehicle. I thought I might be going again to see the water that moved. I felt a tingle of excitement in my tummy thinking about playing on the ground that moved beneath my feet, and which got in between my toes. Eventually, the vehicle stopped. I couldn't smell the water that moved, but then I caught the scent of something on the air. I wasn't sure, but I thought that I could smell the little dog.

They came to the back of the vehicle and attached the loop around my body. I jumped out. I could smell her again but couldn't see her, and then I was *sure* I could smell her. I led them to where I thought the scent came from—from inside a building. Then the front of it opened, and there she was—the dog with the teeth and the lady who smelt like the white sweets. The small dog bounded outside and jumped around my feet. She got in my way and I nearly trod on her, but then she showed me those teeth so I ignored her. I'd seen dogs with much bigger teeth than that!

They put a loop on her and we all went to an area with green grass that sometimes makes my tummy feel sick when I eat it. We had a long walk and then went back to the lady. The dog with the teeth jumped up on the seat beside her. Suddenly she was the same height as me, and we stood eyeball to eyeball. I turned my eyes away from her, as she was quite frightening with her bulging, staring eyes. When she lifted her lips and showed me her teeth again, I knew I was in trouble, and my bravery from earlier was just a distant memory. I stretched and yawned at her and she stopped it, but I knew that it had been a close shave! Later, she curled up on the seat beside me. I wished she would make her mind up about whether I was her friend or not!

They took me to see her a few times, and each time she was the same as before. She just didn't seem to be able to make up her mind about whether she was friendly or not. Still, it was always nice to see her, as I missed seeing her back at my home.

Sometimes when I thought we were going to see her, we didn't go so far. Instead, we ended up in the place where there were many trees, where I could smell many other dogs who were not always there (but I knew they had been).

Sometimes people with dogs on loops stopped nearby. The dogs danced around me, and I danced around them, while the people made noises to each other. I occasionally heard them say "Ralph," and I knew by then that they meant me. I still found it all very confusing. Sometimes the people who were holding onto the other dogs reached out to touch my head, but I wouldn't let them because I remembered what had happened to me before, and I didn't want it to happen again.

One day as I rode in the back of the vehicle, I watched through the darkened window and, high in the sky I saw a creature with wings hovering, and it swooped down onto the ground. Then I couldn't see it anymore. I wondered how it did that. I also saw a big dog on a loop with a smaller dog—like the one with the teeth—beside him, and I wondered where they were going. I don't think they saw me, though. The journey was long and I could feel my legs getting tired, but I carried on standing so I could see what was going on outside. Then the vehicle bumped along much more slowly, until eventually, we stopped.

At first they left me in the back of the vehicle, which I wasn't too pleased about, and I wondered where they had gone. The front of a building opened, and I saw two big dogs come out of it. Then one of my people came out and opened the vehicle where I was, and I cowered as far away as I could get. He caught me with the loop, so I gave up and followed, watching every move he made—just in case.

We went inside the building where those dogs had come from, and I could still smell them. Then I noticed the scent of another dog, and when I saw her, she was the colour of the big, friendly dog. She was showing me a toy that she was carrying in her mouth, which I thought was somewhat strange. She came over and sniffed me, and then I sniffed her back. She smelt of food and those other two dogs. Then she disappeared into another room. I wanted to follow, but I had a loop on. They brought her back to the place where we were all sitting. This time she wasn't paying very much attention to me. She was next to one of the people who smelt of those other dogs. She just sat there, staring at me. I think she was trying to work out what I was doing there. Well, if I'm honest, I was wondering the same thing. I wondered if I was going to be staying there with her—like when I went to the place with the moving water.

They gave some food pieces to her, and then I was offered some. Suddenly, she was there, right next to me, staring straight into my face. However, I took the food and ate it quickly before she could steal it. She was given some more, too, but she obviously wanted to have mine as well as hers. She actually poked her head in front of mine and took some. She was quite forward and very bossy, and I wasn't very sure about her.

After a while, the door to the room opened, and those two dogs who had left earlier came back in. They came right up to me. They were both bigger than I was and looked down at me, and the one who was biggest and a boy like me, wagged his tail. I liked him a lot. The other one put her nose right up to mine and stared into my eyes like the other one had, and I knew straight away not to mess with her. She gave a soft rumble in the back of her throat, and so I swallowed and licked my lips and yawned at her. I breathed a sigh of relief as she went over to her bed and lay there glaring at me. She got up, and so I went to lie where she had been lying. Then I realised everyone was watching me. I wondered what was wrong. The one with the evil stare came right up to my face again, and that rumble started again in her throat. I yawned at her and then looked away. I glanced back at her from the corner of my eye, and she was still there, hovering over me, so I made a quick retreat over to the other side of the room.

Eventually, my people stood up. As the female secured my loop, it became clear that I was going with them, so I stood up, too. I stretched and yawned while I waited to see what was going to happen next. Then the strangest thing happened. They put a band around the greedy one's neck and then put a loop on her as well. I was confused, and even more so when we got outside and she jumped into our vehicle in front of me! I turned to wait for them to tell her to get out, but they didn't. I realised I was going to have to get in there with her, and so, when they gave a gentle tug on the loop, I jumped in next to her. She sighed, but I wasn't sure why. I lay down near to her and turned my back to her, wondering why she was there.

The vehicle started to move. I glanced around and she was still there, so I closed my eyes, as I was feeling quite tired. Then I felt pressure on my lower back. She was resting her head on me! I wasn't having any of that, so I stood up and moved away from her. She sighed again.

She had some toys with her and, for a while, I sat wondering how I could play with them in the back of the vehicle. Eventually I realised it would be too difficult, so I closed my eyes and went back to sleep. The next thing I knew, the vehicle was stopping and I opened my eyes and saw that we were back at home.

I turned around and looked beside me, and she was still there—looking right back at me.

CHAPTER 10

Luella

I joined the family before he did, and suddenly there he was, larger than life. Well, he was certainly much bigger than I was anyway.

They had taken me back to the place they had collected me from, and he stood right beside me, sniffing around me. I was not very amused, I can tell you. I glared up at him to let him know that I wasn't going to take any nonsense from him. No Sirrree, no nonsense from the big, pathetic dogs. I thought for a moment that they were going to replace him for me and leave me there, so I was quite relieved when we all got back in the vehicle. I got the prime position in the back of the car on the middle of the seat where I could reach my head up to see where we were going.

They call me Luella. As far back as I can remember I've been called that, even before they took me on the vehicle that went over the big water. I came here to live with an old lady who gives me human biscuits to eat when she has a hot drink. These are much nicer than dog biscuits, so sometimes I hold out before eating the dog biscuits, just in case there's another of those sweet ones coming my way.

We don't live in the same place as Ralph, but we were staying there for a while when he first arrived. He's so annoying, that dog. He does all this pathetic pretending he's scared so he gets a lot of attention, when really he's a tyrant who, as soon as they're not looking, chases me around the house, pouncing on me at every opportunity he gets. He's been caught doing it sometimes, and they say to him, "Ralphie, leave Luella alone!" But before he leaves me alone, he always tries to flatten me with those enormous paws. I always make the most of it, however, and turn and snarl at him to show him who's in charge.

Sometimes he puts his front end down on the floor, so he's at my level, and keeps his back end in the air (which, if you ask me, looks rather stupid). He stares right into my eyes so we're looking directly at each other, eyeballs to eyeballs. He shouts at me with a very strange bark, which almost sounds like he's shouting his own name. As I said, a tyrant that dog. When he gets ideas above his station, I jump onto the soft seats so I am the same height as him, and then I eyeball him back. That generally sorts him out, especially when I raise my lips and show him my teeth, and then he knows I mean business.

Occasionally he really steps out of line—like when he steals my bouncing ball from under my nose. Those are times when I don't just show him my teeth, but I growl fiercely. If he still doesn't give me my ball back, I have no qualms about snapping at him. That usually works. He is so stupid some-times, though, and just stands there gawping at me. Well, let me tell you, my mouth might be quite small, but my teeth are very sharp.

We all stayed together like that for a while in that building, but then the old woman and me, we went in the vehicle and ended up back at the smaller place where the two of us live. I love it here; it's the best place I've ever been because it's right oppo-site a wide, open space with lots of paths and trees. Many people take their dogs there, and I get to go there several times a day to intimidate them all. I'm much happier in this place, and Ralph comes to see me sometimes. When he doesn't annoy me, I like to show him the big open space. When I see the other dogs, I puff my chest out to show them all who's in charge.

The old woman tried to get me to sleep on a fluffy dog bed when I first arrived here. It was very nice and all that, but not as nice as the big human bed, so I insisted on sleeping there on top of the big blankets. Eventually she let me because she realised I was right.

I am always right.

People come here sometimes to help the old woman, but they get in the way of my routine with their nosing around, making clattering and banging noises in the kitchen, the bathroom, or with the fireplace in the sitting room. I don't like them, because although I think they're there to help the old woman by fixing things, I have a fixed routine these days. I get up, take a big stretch, go for a walk, breakfast, biscuit, go for a walk, food bowl gets topped up, crunchy chew, walk, food bowl gets topped up, out to do my lady-business, supper, out for a walk and more lady-business. I then watch the box in the corner of the room, go out for the last time of the day to do some more private business, and then bed. It's a routine that works for the old woman and me, but when those people come and start clattering, if I don't like them, I show them my teeth. Then for some reason I am put into the bedroom until they've gone away. This is most inconvenient I can tell you. I can still smell them when I come out, though, and I have to search everywhere just to make sure that they've really gone and are not just hiding in the kitchen cupboard or something.

The old woman I live with keeps this bag of doggie goodies hanging from the door handle next to the fridge. All I have to do is follow her into the kitchen and look longingly at the bag and then up at her, making sure I make my eyes as wide as I possibly can. And it's like magic! She immediately reaches inside, pulls something out, and gives it to me. Some of the food in there is better than the rest of it, and I especially like those black biscuits, the ones that are shaped like a bone.

They seemed to be having a clear out in the kitchen one time recently, and the bag of treats disappeared. Well, I was virtually inconsolable, and I could see that the old woman was, too. She was searching all over the kitchen, and I was trying to help, getting more and more distressed by the minute, wondering where the bag had gone. I could sense only a faint smell where it used to be. In the end I heard her speaking loudly on the machine she sometimes speaks into (which I think is an incredibly strange thing to do). Finally, the panic was over, because she opened one of those packets of human biscuits and gave me two of those. Phew, I had thought for a minute I would have to do without my treat.

Lately Ralph's not been over so much, but when his person comes to see the old woman, she takes me to the big space over the road. She sometimes runs alongside me, which is fun, but she's a bit slow and we end up going for a long walk instead. As we walk along the path, she makes this funny repetitive sound in her throat that goes something like, "Loo, Loo, Loo, Luella Looooo." She keeps on saying my name over and over again. Does she think I don't know my own name? She must think I'm a bit stupid or something! Of course I know my own name—and many other things, too. I'm actually very intelligent!

She smells of him, that Ralph, so I know he's still there at that building with her. Lately I've been worried, though, because when she comes to visit she also smells of another dog, and I can't quite figure out what's going on there.

CHAPTER 11

Peggy

Well, what do you think about that?

That dratted dog ran around that track after that furry toy with the long ears. He was behind me, and I thought yes, got it, got it, it's definitely mine! And then, oh my Lord, that dastardly stripy hound just pipped me at the post! Well, I'll be darned, my heart was just about to thud right out of my chest. That little pip-squeak had taken all my glory and they were cheering him and, well, I just stood there watching. They didn't say much, but I could tell they were disappointed with me. I made a secret promise to myself that next time that stuffed bunny toy would be mine—I would guarantee it!

We headed back home to the other dogs, and I was so ashamed. How would I explain this one to the others? However, when I returned they weren't really interested, so I remained huddled in my kennel, hoping the people would take me again so I could show them what I could do. But each time when I thought it was time to go, I didn't get to go with them, and I had to stay behind in the kennel. I was left wondering and promising myself again that when I got to go there, I'd show them all, especially those other dogs who thought they could run faster than I could. I lay and thought about the glory days when I was so popular. Even so, they sometimes took me to run and play with the others, and when this happened I took the opportunity to show them what I could do, and I saw a glimmer of happiness in their eyes. They patted me and said, "Good girl," which made me happy, too.

One day they came to my kennel and I got to go with them to run on the track. And, oh boy, did I ever! I ran faster than I had ever run before—and I was winning! I really was. And then suddenly my front leg twisted. I yelped, but I'm not sure if anyone heard me. It was so sore I had to stop. I couldn't walk without it hurting me. I looked around and everyone was watching me, and that dog behind me was now in front of me. I tried to catch up, but the pain in my leg wouldn't let me. I waited as they all ran past me. I hobbled in behind them, and then I felt strong arms around me. Someone ruffled my ears and they wrapped something around my leg. It felt more secure, but I could still feel it throbbing. They stood around talking while I waited. All I wanted was to go and rest. Eventually they put me in the back of the car and we started back on the long journey home.

I wasn't allowed to go with them to run anymore after that. When they removed the thing they had wrapped around my leg, I was finally let outside to play with the other dogs. I tried to chase them, but it was still very sore. One day, they put me in the car, and we drove for a while until we reached a place I'd never been before. In the distance, I could hear some dogs barking.

A woman who smelt of sweet foods was there. During the day, I lay in a kennel next to another dog, and each day she fed us a couple of times, but I was bored and wanted to go back to where they used to take me to run, as that was all I had ever known. The lady was kind, though, and brought us food that I'd smelt before — the kind of food people used to eat when I'd been racing the other dogs. It was delicious and much better than the food I'd always had in my bowl. When I felt peckish, though, I felt forced into eating the food in the bowl, although it was always a bit of an imposition!

The nights were long, cold, and dark. During the day when we went out for walks with the woman, the ground was hard. I longed for the sunshine to come again. When I slept, I sometimes thought that I was back running with the other dogs and that I was winning. The toy rabbit was right in front of me, and I was happy, jumping around and wagging my tail. Then someone would put a ribbon on me and say, "Good girl." Other times I woke and all I could remember was this large stripy dog. He had big fangs! He would turn to glance at me as we were running side by side, then he would nudge me out of the way, and as he raced past me, I twisted my paw. While I don't remember if that's really what happened back then, I can guarantee that if I ever see that monster of a dog again, then I would give him a piece of my mind, so I would.

And so, that new life became my life. A distant memory now, the racing was over. I lay in the kennel and wondered if that was how things would be from then on. Then one day after I'd had my sweet piece of food from the nice lady who walked us and fed us, the gate opened. Another lady and a man stood in front of me and they came over and started ruffling my ears. I felt myself coming over all shy, but it wasn't like me. They seemed to like this, so I did it some more. They got down to my level and let me sniff their faces. I liked them! They took me for a short walk and then put me in the back of a car that smelt of two dogs I didn't recognise. I didn't know where they were taking me and imagined that maybe they would take me to chase the bunny toy with the long ears. I'd be running again, and then I'd be able to show everyone, including that stripy dog, who the fastest dog in town was once again.

However, we didn't go to the racetrack, we went to a house that smelt of these people, mixed with the scent of two dogs—a male and female. I saw some more people inside the house. Some of them were much smaller, and the smallest one—a female who smelt like fruit and sweets—came and put her arms around me, while the ones who I assumed were her parents told her to be cautious. They pulled her away from me gently, and I understood. Nevertheless, I felt a little put out because I would never have hurt her.

From out of another place in their home, the two dogs I had smelt earlier came bounding over to me. They were both much bigger than I was, and they seemed to recognise what it was like to be like me. While the female was a bit of a snooty madam, and grumbled a little and tossed her head at me, she didn't scare me. The larger male, I think they called "Max", was a gentle old soul. Much, much later the three of us settled down to sleep together, while the family watched a picture moving on a box with a loud noise in the corner. I liked this new life with them and hoped they would let me stay. They seemed to know my name, and I liked the way the young, small female spoke to me gently while she stroked my head. If there was a heaven, then this was surely the doggie heaven I had dreamed of on those dark, cold nights as I had licked at my sore leg.

I loved being with those people. The small female would often come over to me and make a "mwah" sound on the top of my head as she put her arms around my neck. She smelt of a mixture of sweet food and flowers, and I wanted to protect her. There was a man who came home at strange times; he sat by me and let me drape my head across him while we both snoozed. One of the other dogs (the snooty one) was a bit pushy, but I can give as good as I get. Once I got to know her, I just told her with my eyes and she would look away. I knew then that I had won. The bigger, male dog was much easier to get the better of. He would let me take the soft toys out of his mouth and race off with them. I don't think I had ever been that happy before in my whole life.

A man sometimes came and brought paper squares and boxes to the door, and I used to race the other dogs to the door whenever I heard the noise it made, which meant he was there. This became a part of our routine, and sometimes I beat them to the door. It felt like I had won the race, and I imagined that everyone was cheering for me.

One day they both rushed by me and got there first. As they both stood there with their lolling tongues hanging out of their mouths, the rotten scoundrels, I waited for them further back in the hall, ready to ambush them when they came past me.

But it wasn't the man with the boxes.

A male and female human walked in and made their way through to the room where we kept our beds. This was where we went to sit to eat food and watch the box in the corner. As I wasn't too keen on strangers, I disappeared into the other room out of the way. I went to collect my toy, but then changed my mind and just stayed with it in the back room. I was sure they would go away very soon.

I could hear them communicating. It didn't sound threatening, so I sneaked to the edge of the doorway and looked. When I sniffed the air, the man who came home at odd hours of the night and day called me, "Peggy, Peggy. Here she is. Come here, girl."

Reluctantly, I went in. The strangers appeared not to have left yet, and they seemed friendly enough, so I went over to greet them. They gave me some treats, which made me like them. They smelt of a dog, a male dog. The other two dogs came over to smell, too.

The younger members of the family appeared with some leads, and we all got excited. However, it soon became very clear they were only taking the other two, and that I was staying there to entertain the 'guests'. I decided to stick with the man I knew and rested my head on his arm. He seemed to like that because it made him stroke my head. Out of the corner of my eye, I watched the visitors. Eventually they got up and walked to the door, but I wasn't sure whether I should follow them out of the room. Before I knew what was happening, lo and behold, back they came with the dog I had been able to smell on them.

He was about my size. When he saw me, he raised his head a few inches, which made him appear taller. But I wasn't fooled! He had the strangest ears I'd ever seen in my whole life—and I've seen a lot of dogs' ears, so I knew precisely what I was talking about. Normal dogs have their ears folded back; in fact, all the dogs I have known have them like that because it makes them run faster. I couldn't see mine, but I knew that I held them back, as I have to admit that it takes a little effort to do so. Now and then, if I'm out for a walk and I spot one of those furry creatures like the ones I saw when I used to run, I get a little excited, and forget myself and my ears flick up to the top of my head. It does take a little concentration to keep them folded back. With those big ears moving as he walked, he was taken through to the place with the noisy box that they watch, and I couldn't take my eyes off him as the aforementioned ears bounced on top of his head. I found this incredibly distracting.

They shut the door so I couldn't go through to the other room. The one who was holding the dog with the funny ears, who, I gathered, was called "Ralph," called me over. I caught a whiff of Ralph, and he smelt okay. The other 'guest' got down on the floor beside me. She talked to me and offered me a piece of food, so I liked her even more.

I like my food.

She stroked the top of my head and looked into my eyes. While everyone talked, I went back over to the other side of the room to the people I knew. Shortly after, the door opened, and the other two dogs came bounding back in. Ralph seemed quite frightened and, for a moment, it made me feel like I should look after him, just as I looked after my Teddy. He seemed pleased to see the other two, but he was quite unsure of himself. He made his way over to the bed by the window and I thought, "Uh-oh, BIG mistake," but very surprisingly, the one they call Millie let him lie there. Well, you could have blown me over with a duster, or whatever it is they say, because had I done that she'd have been on my case straight away. However, that dog just curled up into a ball and, what's more, she just watched him.

But then, oh yes, that was more like it. She sidled up next to the bed and hovered over him, growling at him, and the low rumble in her throat got louder until those silly ears of his finally took in what was happening. He got up and slinked back over to the one who was holding him on the lead. I really didn't think that the Millie one would put up with his lying on her bed.

The treats were coming thick and fast. Ralph took them sometimes, but he had this very strange habit of not taking them properly when he was offered them. He just knocked them onto the floor with his nose and then picked them up from the carpet to eat. I wasn't sure where he had learned his manners, but I thought he needed to learn a lesson or two. The next time he did it, I leaped forward and picked it up from the floor before he could get it. Ha! That showed him. It was a good game. Speaking of manners, I noticed he had this annoying habit of yawning at me. Well, it wasn't just me he was yawning at. No, not at all! He was yawning at everything, and I mean EVERYTHING—the people, the other dogs, and even the chair. The chair for heaven's sake! What an absolutely peculiar dog.

I wondered when they were going to leave.

Then I noticed that something was up, and the dog known as Ralph was getting his lead on, which would have been fine, as I had been wondering when he was going, but there was a snag! It looked as though I was going with him. I expected it would be for a walk and that would have been okay because I could have shown him where the local rabbits were. Suspecting it was something more, I thought to myself, "Well, no one asked me what I thought about this," as I watched Ralph yawn at the door.

As we stood by the door ready to go out, Millie and Max looked at me in a knowing way. I wasn't sure whether they were pleased or not. Then the girl from the house came up to me, but I couldn't quite gauge what she was thinking. She said my name, touched my head with her face, and held me tight. Her mouth smelt of sweet biscuits and her hair of fruit. She seemed sad, and I wanted to stay there with her forever.

Once outside, we walked past some cars and the family from the house stood back by the door, watching us. A car door opened. The man of the house, who had followed us outside, touched me on my head and said my name. I thought that he might have been feeling sad. The man who opened the door to the car gently pulled on my lead, and I got the idea, so I jumped in. Then that Ralph dog jumped in after me.

I had forgotten all about him.

There was a flurry of activity outside. I stood up in the back of the car and wagged my tail as I saw them walking over. "Yes, yes, they are coming back to get me," I thought.

The door at the front of the car opened, and they passed in my squeaky toys and Ted, the furry toy I carried around in my mouth on those rare occasions when I wasn't quite sure of myself. The female in the front of the car took them, and then the engine started up. So, I was leaving after all. I sighed as I lay down again. I could see Ted in the front of the car, and all I wanted was to pick him up and have him in the back of the car with me. I rested my head on Ralph's back, at which he turned and looked at me as though I had three heads. He promptly got up and moved as far away from me as the back of the car would allow. I felt bad for finding his ears so amusing, but it was too late for that. I closed my eyes and hoped I would wake up back in the house with the little girl who hugged my head.

The woman in the front kept on turning around and pulling that face that I've learned is a happy face, as nice things usually happen when people pull that face. She seemed kind and so did the man who was sitting next to her, but I really felt that whatever was going on, someone should have considered what I had thought about it!

The journey lasted for a while, and then we stopped. While we waited to get out of the car, floppy-eared Ralph (I told myself I must stop looking at those ears and must see beyond them, as he might actually be a very nice dog) glanced at me as though he wasn't sure why I was there. I have to admit, that that made two of us.

Inside the house was the faint smell of other dogs. I could smell at least two, but there may have been more. I saw only Ralph, though. They kept me on the lead and walked me around the house. I couldn't quite figure out what was going on, but they kept on calling my name and bringing Ralph over to see me. He jumped up on the big seat, and I was very impressed that he could get away with it. I figured I would try that myself later on. For the time being, though, there were more important issues to deal with…

Food.

There were treats galore and, once they removed the lead, I willingly followed them around, eagerly taking each morsel they offered. Ralph was a bit slower at taking his, so I stole them quite deftly from under his nose and hoped that no one would notice. The people seemed to think this was amusing, and I assumed I must have been doing something right, so I did it again a few times. On the next offering, however, I noticed they gave me just one morsel, while Ralph got several. They blocked me from making a beeline for his and he got extra time to eat them.

It had been quite a busy day. I started to wonder when (or if) I would be going back to the other house. Later on, they attached some double band thing around my chest like a huge collar; they'd also attached something metal to the collar around my neck. When I walked it jingled, and I quite liked the sound it made. I'd seen other dogs with them on and always wondered what it would be like to have one of my own. I noticed that Ralph had one too, and it made the same sound. Once they'd trussed me up like a parcel in this contraption around my chest, they attached a lead, and we were off. I headed over to the car, but they gently tugged on the lead. We were going for a walk instead. Well, I thought, at least that made up for the one I had missed earlier on.

My impression of Ralph being most peculiar intensified as I watched him leap up and down on the end of his lead whenever he saw anything that moved. And I mean anything—cars, which I think he's quite scared of, those long-eared rabbit creatures, of which there were many around these parts, and cats, those awful creatures with the evil eyes and the sharp claws. I knew they were sharp because I had been on the receiving end of them on more than one occasion.

At the end of the walk, we returned to the house. After we rested on the nice, soft beds in the room with the talking box (what is it with people and those talking boxes?), Ralph and I were given a bowl of food in raised food bowls. I was glad they raised it up off the floor, as I got awful indigestion if I had to put my head right down to the floor when I was eating. It was then time for another rest. Later, I was lying in a deep sleep dreaming of racing around a track and I was woken up. It was time to go for another walk.

Lordy, did these people never rest?

There were a lot of steps in the house, and they seemed to go on forever. Ralph took great pleasure in standing on the steps and beckoning me with his playful eyes several times before I finally decided to follow him. I'd decided he was a bit of a character, that one. It must have been bedtime because it was dark outside and everyone was yawning—especially Ralph, who I thought must have something seriously wrong with him because he yawned constantly.

Reluctantly, I followed them all up the steps and then, once at the top, I made the huge mistake of looking back down. And, oh, my auntie's diamond-studded collar, I went cross-eyed. My head spun as the bottom of the steps seemed to be a hundred feet away. Apparently, we had to go back into the back garden for a pee before we went to the nice comfortable beds I'd spotted in the room where I thought they must sleep. So, down we went, and Ralph, that cheeky, mixed-up pup, raced down in front of me. When we got back inside, he charged through the back door and skidded along the carpet in the kitchen. Meanwhile, I gingerly placed one foot in front of the other as I delicately navigated my way down each step. My front leg was sore and, after all the walking and the stresses of the day, I felt very tired. When we finally made our way to the room up those stairs again, I was so grateful for the comfortable bed beside the place where these people slept. I was delighted when I discovered that I didn't have to squash in next to that Ralph, as it appeared that he had a bed of his own, right next to mine.

The female came over to me and made that squeaking sound like the little female used to. She touched her face to my head, and then she went over to Ralph and did the same. "I could get used to this," I thought to myself, especially when she held her hand out and gave me more tasty morsels. I accepted them without any hesitation—and then tried to make my way across to Ralph to take his, too.

Shattered after the events of the day, I turned on my back, put my legs in the air, and nodded off. Meanwhile, I listened to the calm, soothing breathing sounds as the people and the crazy dog Ralph slept. I hoped that, for once, the dreams of the rabbit that went around and around the track wouldn't dominate my sleep, and that more peaceful images of big, comfortable chairs and food bowls that were never empty would relax me ready for the next day.

Whatever that day would bring.

CHAPTER 12

Us

When eventually I managed to find the time to look at Peggy's racing records (and there were many more than I had ever imagined there would be), I became extremely emotional when I discovered that this sweet, sleek girl—who carries teddies around in her mouth and insists that they live next to the sofa in the back sitting room—is an ex-racing champion. She is the daughter of a very successful racing greyhound—and is one of his many offspring. Her father is now retired and making his "living" as a stud dog.

I was overwhelmed to discover that she had hundreds and hundreds of half brothers and sisters. Somewhere, just from that one sire, there were (or had been) all these dogs that had been bred for their slender shape and ability to run fast. How many of them eventually become successful at racing? How many of those dogs were still living a happy, contented life? I supposed that was the six million dollar question.

A DOG LIKE RALPH

Many years ago when I was working as a student veterinary nurse, someone came in to the practice and asked for his three healthy young greyhounds to be put to sleep because they were no longer any good for the racetrack. I was working at the reception desk at the time and thought initially that he was joking. You know, I had heard it all before, people looking down at their dog or cat and saying things like, "If we end up back here again, it'll be to put you down," when told what their bill was, as they shook their heads in horror at the cost of the treatment. Invariably, this statement was followed by the owner leaning forwards and plonking a great big kiss on top of their pet's head.

Those people with their pampered pets had never meant it, but this time it was for real and, in spite of it being suggested that the dogs should be rehomed, the owner insisted. He said that if we didn't put them to sleep, then he would find someone else who would. So he went to wait in the waiting room because, although he didn't want to see them die, he intended to come back through to the clinic to check that the awful deed had been done. And so, one by one, those dogs died in my arms.

That was over thirty years ago, and similar scenes are played out in veterinary practices in the western world time and time again, even today. In that time, welfare groups have campaigned endlessly about changing the law to make the trade in greyhounds more restrictive, however, just as with other dogs, there are too many of them for the number of owners available, and so greyhounds join the masses in pursuit of a loving home.

Each dog who is born is a dog who needs to have a home, and for each dog, with a little luck, it will be a forever home. However, rescue shelters are bursting at the seams with all kinds of dogs, not just greyhounds. There are people out there who are breeding so many litters of dogs of all types who, for the most part, are serving an industry made up of short-term fancies and whims. There is a lot of outright exploitation of the dogs going on by many who are involved in breeding them.

There are happy endings, though, and for all the sad, sad stories, there is a multitude of cases where dogs have ended up living full and contented lives. I hope this is the case for Peggy and Ralph. As humans, we watch our dogs, and we never really know whether they're truly happy. We watch their behaviour and note that they wag their tails; we give them a companion so they're not alone when we have to leave them for a few hours, and we talk to them so the bond between us is strengthened. We hope that we're doing the right things for them and that, above all else, they are content with their lot.

Peggy has an old racing ligament injury to her left forelimb, and one of her toes is elevated above the other three. When we first got her, she walked with a profound limp. Our veterinary surgeon recommended anti-inflammatory painkillers, which she will need to take for the rest of her life, and she is only just approaching middle age. These painkillers have several long-term side effects, including kidney or liver failure and stomach ulcers. With this in mind, and to minimise these side effects, we have her on the lowest effective dose, a dose that will need to be administered to her forever, perhaps increasing in old age. I guess that's something that she has to live with as an ex-racer—she, and many thousands of dogs like her. They become injured, and they're of no use anymore. In some cases, they are (if they're the luckier ones, as so many fall foul to horrific outcomes) given to greyhound rescue charities. Then people like me find their picture on a rescue web page, read their description, and consider how their personality and the little quirks that have been discovered while they've been with their foster home or in kennels would suit our lifestyle and the other animals in the household.

The information given about each dog varies between animal shelters, and will depend on what they've managed to discover but, generally, the list goes something like the following—and is usually accompanied by a series of ticks or noncommittal 'unknowns':

Cat-friendly?
Dog-friendly?
Small dog-friendly?
Child friendly?
House-trained?
Good in car?

Where dogs have been in foster homes, it enables potential owners to find out a little more about the dog and about how she or he interacts with others. In most cases with rescue dogs, however, you are generally working with very little information.

Peggy's description stated that she was a calm, friendly dog and that she was good on the lead. All of this is true about her, because she is a lovely dog, and just what we had been looking for in terms of a companion for Ralph and ourselves. Her picture on the website didn't do her justice, which didn't worry us as her personality was far more important to us than how she looked, and we expected to be meeting a dog who was not very attractive. However, when we first set eyes on her, we saw that she was quite beautiful. She has sleek, black fur, which is dappled with fine, white flecks along her back, and the profile of her muzzle is such that her shiny black nose extends beyond the line of her lower jaw, giving the impression of an extremely long, pointed face. She has gorgeous black upper eyelashes framing her velvet, dark brown eyes, which she flutters at you as she passes by with her teddy—which has invariably been moved from its allocated position in the dining room by her sometime adversary, Ralph!

Peggy doesn't have the air of a dog who has been hurt by people. She has a confidence that I've only ever seen in one of our other previous adult rescue dogs, Dillon. Dillon had clearly been cared for by his first owners, and I'm sure the reason they had to give up on him was a genuine one. I've always imagined that it was something they couldn't avoid doing because of whatever their personal circumstances were. I would go as far as saying that Dillon had been very much loved in his previous home.

I'm positive of that. While I don't think that Peggy had received that same level of love, I certainly don't think she was mentally or physically hurt in a deliberate way by her racing owner. Her injuries are because of her racing, not because of how her owner treated her per se. Ralph bears many emotional scars, and although I'm sure Peggy's life was not altogether easy with the hand she was dealt in her younger years, I have no doubt that she fared better than he did.

So many dog charities would not be able to cope without the dedication and hard work of their armies of volunteers, and Peggy, having been handed over to the charity by her racing owner, found herself in kennels for several months. The time that she spent there included some of the coldest weather conditions that the UK had seen in many decades. When she was taken by the charity, there was no space in any of the foster homes, but then she finally made it into a foster home with a lovely family who took great care of her and integrated her into their busy lives, along with their own two greyhounds. It was this wonderful family we visited on that cold, wet July day in order to go and see Peggy for the first time.

We took Ralph with us on the seventy-five mile journey to meet his potential new companion. For a short while, he stayed outside in the car, while we went in the house to chat to Peggy's 'foster parents'. We were so excited to at last meet this good-natured dog we'd read about on the rescue web page. In order to arrive at the conclusion that

Peggy was the one for us, and more importantly a good, solid friend for Ralph, we had drawn up a short list. In every way, she had come out on top. We had decided that a bitch would be better than a dog because we felt that Ralph would be a lot less likely to feel threatened by a female. We also felt sure that the dog we got would have to be older than Ralph, as he still had a huge degree of puppyishness about him. I guess in some ways, quite subconsciously, we were looking for some kind of surrogate mother for Ralph—a dog who could show him how to behave like a dog and show him that, for the most part anyway, people were not to be feared.

When Oskar had been fading fast, we reflected a lot on what we had been through in the year leading up to his worsening. Having lost Dillon and Charlie in such quick succession—and not wanting to accept that Oskar was unlikely to see the holiday we had booked to take him on—there had been a lot of soul searching. We had decided that when we did eventually bring more animals into our lives, we would never again want to be in the position whereby all our animals were old at the same time. So, by having an age gap between them, even though there were no guarantees that they would necessarily go in the order dictated by their ages, we felt that we'd minimise the risk of having all that heartbreak happening again in one go.

On entering the hallway of Peggy's fosterers, we were greeted by a huge blue and white male greyhound and a smaller black and white bitch.

They were the fostering family's own two dogs. But there, lurking in the background, and a little apprehensive, was the gorgeous and slightly smaller black and white greyhound who we assumed was Peggy. She was shrinking away and hiding at the back of the hall, while the other two dogs were full-on, demanding our attention. She didn't come through to see us straight away, but when she did, it was clear that even though she had only been with her foster family for just over a week, she was really happy with them. In fact, they told us that she had settled in so well that they had considered keeping her.

The children of the family took their own two dogs for a walk, while we brought Ralph in to meet Peggy, at which, she immediately disappeared into the other room. He wanted to play and clearly, he liked her, but she was not interested. She was obviously put out at not having been taken for a walk with the other two dogs. She went through to the other room, apparently to sulk. Her foster 'dad' went through and brought her back in, and once the two dogs were together, it was clear that she was happy with Ralph being around. We sat and chatted with her foster parents for a while and let the two dogs get to know each other. We were desperate to take her home, and having already been through all the usual home checks, we waved good-bye to this lovely family and set off with the two dogs secured in the car.

We had put the back seats down in the back of the car to give the dogs a lot of space, and this meant we could keep an eye on them during the journey. As we set off, they both lay down. Looking as though she needed a little reassurance, Peggy reached over and rested her head on Ralph's lower back. Immediately he turned to look at her as if to say, "You're a bit forward aren't you?" and stood up and went and lay down about six inches away from her with his back to her—just far enough for her not to be able to do it again.

I felt so sorry for this poor, pretty greyhound who had been through so much and who was suddenly in a car with two people she had never met before, and a dog who was clearly not interested in having her anywhere near him. My heart lurched as she rested her head between her long front paws and she let out a deep sigh. She had gone from being a dog who was transported to and from racetracks, to living in an outdoor kennel for several months, to living for a short time with her foster family (and had obviously settled in with them), to being transported to a life with us she would hopefully enjoy. At that moment, however, she must have wondered what on earth was going on.

She was beautiful and I loved her immediately. Her maturity was evident compared to Ralph, and I felt that we had definitely made the right decision in choosing her. There really was a calmness and gentleness about her, and throughout the seventy-five mile journey home, I couldn't take my eyes off these two lovely dogs. I felt that once again our family was complete. Dogs make a home a special place in which to be, and in the year leading up to this point, I had felt our lives dissolving around us as, one by one, our three dogs passed away. Somehow, I had felt a loss of stability.

Animals help to make us whole, and here once again at another juncture in my life, I found myself wallowing in the anticipated joy of the years to come that would be spent loving and nurturing these two lovely creatures.

CHAPTER 13

Ralph

Peggy, that appeared to be what they called her, came back to the building where we all live, so I thought I had better show her where everything was. As we entered through the front door and they removed the bands from around my chest, I glanced over at her. She seemed very shy. She hadn't been like that before. Once I was free of the bands, I spotted that the door to the back of the house was open, so I raced as fast as I could to show Peggy how agile I was. Just when I thought how impressed she would be, I caught the edge of the mat and went sliding across the back room floor, almost ending up falling out of the back door.

I wondered if she had followed me (and more importantly whether she had seen what had happened), but she was still on the loop. I was a little disappointed as I thought that maybe she wasn't going to stay, and that she would disappear to the other place where the small dog with the teeth had disappeared. But I carried on into the back garden anyway. Then she was there with the people, still on the loop, having a wander about. I wasn't sure what was happening, so I yawned a few times, had a few stretches, and continued to watch. They said, "Ralph," a few times, so I went a bit closer—but not too close, just in case—and then she crouched down and peed. This was very interesting, so when they moved away, I went and had a sniff at it, as we dogs do.

Later on when we went out for a walk, I could see that she wasn't scared of the vehicles. I wondered why because they were very, very frightening—especially the big ones with lots of wheels and the smaller loud ones with only a couple of wheels (which sounded a bit like that loud thing that the one who gives me the most face hugs blows her hair with each morning). When we walked on the part of the path that was most busy, I tried to get past the walls as soon as possible so I could avoid the vehicles, but this Peggy was obviously much braver than I was.

Back at the place where we live, we headed up the steps, as it was time to go to sleep, or rather, *the rest of us* headed up the stairs, while Peggy stood at the bottom, looking up. Then I remembered that I had done this too, so I ran back down the steps and up again to show her that it was easy. She eventually, very carefully, tiptoed up the steps. I noticed something wrong with one of her feet—she seemed to be sore. It made me think of my face, and I wondered if that was what had happened to her, too. Eventually she got to the top, and then it seemed that it wasn't time to go to bed after all. We had to go back down again to go outside before we went to bed. I knew what that was for, so I headed down the steps so I could race into the back garden to have a pee up against my favourite tree.

Peggy didn't follow me. I glanced back up to the top of the steps. Peggy looked as though she was swaying a little. I remembered when I did that, and it was not a nice feeling. Eventually she did follow me and, after we'd both had a pee, we all headed back up the steps. They'd put another bed next to mine for Peggy, although I think it might have been nice for her to have shared mine because I think she might not have minded if we had touched toes in the night. Even the big dog at the place with lots of dogs used to let me do that.

Peggy seemed to be extremely happy that we got extra treats at bedtime. She ate hers quickly and then tried to get mine. She is an extremely greedy dog.

The next day we had some nice walks. I liked having another dog to walk alongside; I really liked that she wasn't frightened of the vehicles. It made me think that I could be a bit braver, too. She also wasn't afraid of people. I couldn't understand why, as so many people were very frightening to me. I couldn't work out whether people were more frightening than vehicles, or whether it was the other way around. The people we live with who take us out for walks, feed us and let us sleep in their room seemed to be okay, but you can never be too sure.

I shy away from everyone when they try to touch my head, even the big male person in the house, but he always just ruffles my ears anyway. I have been kind of getting used to it, so I try not to shy away from him so much anymore. When the other people are not there, I sometimes go to lie in his room while he's working and tapping away at some machine in the corner. Since Peggy arrived, she goes to lie there, too. In fact, she not only lies on the big bed, she goes and lies right on the softest part where the people usually put their heads, which I think is a bit cheeky of her.

That leg that I noticed before, I began to realise it really bothered her. I didn't know what she had done to it, but it looked as though it was something quite bad. The female in the house used to rub it for her sometimes, and Peggy lay and let her do it. Sometimes she even let out a soft sigh. I think it helped her.

One day we went on quite a long walk past a place where I saw lots of long-eared creatures hiding in the grass, and Peggy saw them too, but she didn't try to get closer to them like I always did. I thought it was probably because she was more interested in her leg, which had been getting quite bad. Then eventually we were back on a road again, and there were lots of vehicles and buildings. We came to a building that I remembered from before, but I couldn't quite think why. Then, much too late, and before I could do anything about it, I realised what it was. As soon as I got inside the building, I decided I wanted to leave so I pulled back on the loop, but it was no good. I was back at the place where I had got the pain between my back legs. Peggy was behind me, so there was no way to get out. I saw her pull back too, but she was too late as well. It must have been that sore leg that was slowing her down.

The door closed behind us.

And so, we sat and waited in a room with other dogs. There was one like the big, black dog from the place where there were lots of dogs, and there was another much smaller, fluffy dog with very long ears. On the floor was a cage, and inside there was one of those animals that stares out from underneath bushes or vehicles, and sometimes pounces out at me with their sharp claws. I was glad that he was behind the bars because he was glaring at me. I glanced away from him, and when I looked back, he was still staring, so I yawned and put my paws forward and stretched. When I glanced back at him again, he was still staring at me, so I looked away from him and willed myself not to look at him again.

Eventually, he was picked up in his cage and carried over to the other side of the room, and they followed someone through a door. I watched the back of the cage until I couldn't see them anymore—just in case that animal escaped and came to get me.

The big, black dog was getting excited and woofed at any other animal that came into the room, until finally a female came and fetched him. That seemed to shut him up. One by one, the animals followed someone into a room, and then someone came for us. I could feel my body go tense. There were strange smells, and I winced as I remembered what had happened to me the last time I was there. In fact, I had a very strong urge to cross my legs.

There was a man in the room who crouched down beside me. The female person I live with was holding on to me tight and I felt secure, but I could feel something pounding in my chest. The man got hold of something that was shiny and put it into my ear. It was cold, so it made me jump a little. I wished that he would go away, but then he moved to the other side of me and did the same to my other ear. My ears had been very itchy and he was not really helping the issue very much. He left me alone and went over to Peggy. I could see that she was not very sure about what was going on. Perhaps she was wishing that she had crossed her legs before she had gone in there, too.

He put the cold, shiny thing into her ears. She didn't look very impressed, as her eyes went a bit cross-eyed like they always do when she's not sure about something. I was just glad that I was off the hook. Outside the door, I could hear a scuffle of feet, so I sniffed beneath it. It was that big black dog. Well, whatever had happened to him, it had certainly shut him up. Then I started to get worried because maybe they'd do whatever they did to him to me. The female human I lived with was stroking my head, and it comforted me a little. I think they call her "Mmm", because whenever she's near me, I hear them speak something that sounds like, "Mmm," and she says it sometimes when she's putting her head on top of mine and making the squeaking sound. Only, when she does that, she says something like, "Mmmsboy."

Peggy looked even more worried because the man was moving her legs. He seemed to be very interested in the leg that was sore, and she winced a couple of times with the pain. When he stood up, he went and fetched a food treat from the other side of the room. She took it from him. He then came over to me. I wasn't sure about him, so even though it smelt good, I knocked it off his hand and then ate it from the floor. He gave us both another one, and Peggy took hers. I tried to be brave, but I accidentally knocked my next one with my teeth, and it ended up on the floor anyway, so I ate it from there. Needless to say, Peggy tried to get mine, too, but I got it before she did. I was learning.

When we got back to the building where we live, we were just settling down after our food when Mmm and the man came over with some kind of smelly substance that they put into my ear. Then they did the same with the other ear. It really, really smelt of something I'd never smelt before, and I didn't like it. They did the same to Peggy, and then she was given something inside her mouth. They held her jaws together and held her head up while they stroked her throat. Once that was done, they had a look inside her mouth. I remembered having something similar done to me before, but I couldn't remember when. Over the following days, this became a bit of a routine. Sometimes it happened more than once in the day, but then strangely, my ears stopped itching. Then, one day, they didn't put any of the foul-smelling substance in my ears, and I was glad. Peggy still had to have those things that they put into her mouth, though.

Mmm goes out in the vehicle lots of days, but when she is gone, the tall male is often here. Sometimes there's a female with him, and she's nice and lets me cuddle up beside her. The one who sleeps a lot when everyone else is up and the light is on in the sky is here a lot too when Mmm isn't, and he gets down on the floor next to me and talks to me. Sometimes I remember what happened before, and I think about the pain I had on my face. Then I realise that it's not the same as before, and I get confused. He takes me out on the loop a lot, and the tall one sometimes comes too, but most times it's Mmm who comes for walks with him, Peggy, and me.

My favourite place is the place where the two-wheeled vehicles sometimes go whizzing past, and some of them ring a little bell, which is good because then we can stand by and let them go past us so that I don't get scared. Often there aren't any of them about, and we can go for really long walks down there without being disturbed. We see a lot of dogs of all sizes and some that don't even look like dogs. I've seen a couple of really small ones that look really strange—it's as if they've walked into a wall and squashed their faces. They pant a lot, and their tongues hang right out of their mouths. They also make funny noises when they breathe. I don't know whether I want to play with them or not. I think they are really only pretending to be dogs.

The dogs I really love are the ones who wag their tails at me when I go past. Sometimes I bow down to greet them, and occasionally their people make funny noises and show their teeth when they look at me, which I think is strange. But I think it's a happy noise.

When we go out at night, there's a dog we see sometimes who has a flashing collar. It kind of makes me feel nervous, but she's often with another dog who's like the big black one who used to let me touch his paws with my toes—but he's a much lighter shade. This one just ignores me, but I think that he is quite old and doesn't see me very well. I've also seen two dogs that are very big, and they have very pointed ears and stern faces. I don't make eye contact with them. Their people hold them tight on their loops, and I'm glad, because the sooner they move away the better. I try to hide behind Peggy, but I think she's just as worried about them because she skips past on the opposite side of the footpath without looking at them.

The dog I really don't like is another one that is a lot like the dog who used to let me touch his feet with my toes, only this one is quite rude because whenever I see him, he makes a beeline for my privates. All of us dogs do it to a certain degree, but he is very forward, and I really don't like him very much. Peggy hasn't met him yet, but when she does, I suspect she'll sort him out.

Mmm comes home a lot smelling like the little dog with the teeth, so I know that she's still around—probably with the lady with the white sweets that smell like that plant. Although she's not very nice to me, I miss that little dog.

Autumn

CHAPTER 14

Luella

They carried on coming to see me smelling of that dog Ralph, and at one point, it felt like I hadn't seen him for ages. Nevertheless, every time I saw them, they smelt strongly of him and this other dog whose scent I couldn't quite place. The only thing I could tell for sure was that it came from a female like me.

The day started as usual with the old woman letting me out to do my private business. Then she went through her usual ritual of spending a lot of time in the kitchen making a drink, and then coming back through to sit on the seat next to me where she waved this black object in the air in front of her, so the noisy box in the corner would start to speak. After we'd sat there for a while, she'd go and put some different clothes on. And then we'd go for a walk. We didn't go far, though, which was a little disappointing, but I did appreciate going out to see the other dogs.

Virtually every day we have the same routine, except some days she tends to rush around like some crazy woman, and she pushes this noisy object around the floor frantically, while I stay up on the seat well out of the way. When I realised that this appeared to be one of those days, I got a lurch of excitement in my tummy. I might get one of those extra-long walks because they might be coming to see me—the ones who always smell of Ralph.

Later on, the one who comes and sees us on his two-wheeled vehicle arrived and took me to the park for a nice walk. I thought that maybe I was mistaken, and perhaps Ralph's people weren't coming that day. Don't get me wrong. I do appreciate him taking me for a walk, but I see a lot of him. I quite like it when the others come and take me out instead. It makes a nice change in my routine.

So there we were, sitting there, and they were having a cup of tea and a sweet biscuit. I was given one shaped like a bone. I was thinking to myself, "How can I wangle one of those sweet ones?" when the old lady said something I didn't quite catch. Then I realised that they were here; they had come to take me out after all. Almost beside myself with excitement, I dashed to the door and waited. I'd like to say that I waited patiently, but in true Luella-style, I leaped up and down in a vertical fashion as I balanced on my hind legs and wagged my tail so that it was almost too painful to wag it anymore. Occasionally I stopped and sniffed under the door. Yes, yes, I was right! They had come to see me after all. But wait—what was that smell? There was a stronger than usual scent of Ralph and then, once the old woman had finally put the right key in the lock, the door opened and there he was. Or, should I say, there THEY were? For alongside Ralph was the dog I had been smelling on Ralph's people for some time.

Her long, black, pointed face reached forward. She sniffed me and then, in a total lack of interest in me, or what I had to say about her, she tossed her head and looked in the opposite direction. Naturally, Ralph was overjoyed to see me, and we touched noses. He wagged his tail a lot, so I felt obliged to reciprocate, which was a nice moment, if a little embarrassing, as I saw Ben from the park walk past and knew that my reputation would never be the same again. So, I decided to add a little rumble of a growl to my Ralph greeting repertoire, just so he'd know his place.

They attached the rope to the band around my neck and off we went. I felt a little put out, though, because this was my special time. As we wandered down the path next to the trees, I took the opportunity to jump up at Ralph and try to nip him on his neck. He flinched out of the way and then glanced at me weirdly and tossed his head. "A right pair of pals these two are," I thought to myself, as I made sure I was in front of them. Long legs they may have, but this was my walk, and I wasn't going to let them ruin it for me.

A gale blew through the trees, and Ralph's ears flapped in the wind as he trotted along beside me. I took the opportunity to glance past him to the creature he had brought with him. She was tall and long, and I don't think I had ever seen such a narrow, thin face on a dog; she looked quite stern, and she worried me a little, which was very unlike me. As she panted, I stole a look at her teeth. I gulped when I saw them, as they were long, bright, white, and very sharp—and they gleamed in the sun. So that was what he'd done; he'd swapped me for a much bigger version, one with gigantic teeth. I felt like having another go at Ralph, but he was too far away from me and anyway, that big, thin, black dog had clocked me looking at her, so I thought I had better not.

Back at the place where I live with the old woman, things got even worse because it seemed as though Ralph and his new best friend were sticking around for a while. So they came in, and you'd never guess what happened next—I had to share my biscuits with them! My eyes nearly popped out of my head. That tall, black one ate hers and immediately looked for more, which I thought was very much out of order. It was about time I put them right about their behaviour, so I did one of my vertical jumps onto the seat beside the old woman and stood eyeball to eyeball with that long dog. I showed her my teeth, and she looked right back at me. Well, at least I think it was right at me; it was difficult to see both her eyes at the same time as she had this big, long muzzle in the way. But anyway, she eyeballed me, and I could see Ralph in the background getting ready to do one of his stupid snorts. She lifted her head and looked the other way.

"Charming!" was all I could think, especially when the old woman, who was meant to be MY old woman, I might add, reached over and stroked her—yes, HER, on the head and said, "Good girl."

Shortly after they'd eaten my biscuits, it appeared that they were leaving. I went and stood underneath Ralph and looked up at the thin-faced one. She had seen it, I knew she had, and I watched her as she extended her neck over to get a closer look at it. It was a toy that was shaped like a ball, but it had arms and legs, which I had always thought was a little ludicrous. Who ever thought of a ball having arms and legs?

I had never actually paid any attention to it, but that was not the point. I was determined that she was NOT having it! If she got any closer to it, I would let her know that it was out of bounds because I had been given it and, even if I didn't particularly like it, it was mine! I think they must have realised, though, because just as I thought she was going to grab it, one of her humans held her back and said, "No, Peg," or something like that.

Much as it was nice to see Ralph, I was actually quite relieved when, shortly after that incident, he took his new girlfriend away.

CHAPTER 15

Peggy

We went out for a ride in the car and ended up at a building I'd never visited before. When I sniffed the air, I realised that this was the smell that the lady of the house came back smelling of when she went away sometimes. Not only that, the smell reeked strongly of dog and, right enough, the door opened and out came a tiny creature, which could just about be classed as a dog. She was brown like the creatures I used to chase around that track. That got me a little excited as I figured if she ran, I could maybe chase her. I pricked my ears forward, and she looked at me and looked away. Meanwhile, Ralph was wagging his tail at her. He doesn't wag it very often, so she was honored by this spectacle. Still, she responded with a growl and wagged her tail at the same time. "What an ever so curious creature," I thought.

They took us to a place with a lot of grass, and it was so windy that Ralph nearly learned how to fly with those gigantic ears. Meanwhile, the little dog marched in front of us all, showing us where to go, but I thought that was obvious because there were paths along the grassy slopes. We eventually headed back inside away from the howling wind, and once in there a lady gave us some treat biscuits. "Well," I thought to myself, "instant friends indeed." I would definitely come back to see her again. That little dog was standing on the seat, however, showing her teeth to Ralph, while Ralph just stood there, totally oblivious to everything as usual.

We were on our way out when I spotted it, as there on the shelf was a dog toy. I reached over to grasp it with my teeth, only I felt a slight tug on the lead, and they muttered something. I got the picture, "not allowed," I thought to myself, while the little dog stood back up on the big chair, hovering over everyone and flashing her tiny teeth. We made a quick exit after that, and after popping to the grass to go to the toilet, we were on our way home again, leaving the vicious little dog with the old lady.

As for Ralph, he is the strangest dog I have ever met. He has this grossly annoying habit of waiting for me to spend a penny in the garden while he gets into a pouncing position, crouching down with his eyes focused on my face (and sometimes on my rear end, which is more than a little unsettling). I deliberately pretend I haven't noticed him and then, as soon as I've relieved myself, he's there, in my face, winding me up so that I'll chase him. And chase him I do, as it's only what he deserves. I chase him around the place where they grow their food, but then when he thinks he can get away from me,

I turn and cut him off as he comes back around in front of the potatoes. He's so stupid, he doesn't even realise I'm going to do it, even though I do it every time. I then grab him around the neck and show him who the boss is around here.

He's funny, though. He can be like that, all excitable and racing around the house or garden. Then at other times—and I've still not figured out when or why—he's like a quivering wreck, cowering away from the people in the house. I've tried to show him that there's nothing to worry about by going up to them and resting my head on their laps and barking at them in that way that only I can. They really are quite harmless, and I try to let him know that it's okay to communicate with them.

Yes, my bark. I'm glad I've mentioned that, as I'm particularly proud of it because I have perfected it so that it's kind of a cross between a howl, a bark, and a yelp. It's a loud, high-pitched, "yip." I have seen grown men cover their ears when I'm feeling particularly communicative.

Thankfully, Ralph's yawning seems to be getting less, although his favourite 'yawn objects' appear to be the lead, the sofa, and treats. He still does it a lot at people. Whenever we go for a walk, he insists on having a stretch as soon as we get out to the front of the house. If there's a lot of traffic about, he extends this to two, sometimes three, stretches—all followed by a deep yawn. Meanwhile, I stand there waiting for him to sort himself out, which can try a girl's patience. He still licks his lips and stretches a lot, but I think that, overall, he's a lot bolder than when I first came to live here with them. He used to go for a sneaky pee up against the large yucca tree in the room which has all the windows, and that was quite embarrassing. "I hope they don't think that was me!" was my initial reaction. When they noticed, though, they just cleaned it up and didn't say a word to either of us about it. Then later, when we were out for a walk and we did our business, they were ecstatic and practically jumping up and down with joy saying, "Good boy!", which I assume they were saying to Ralph and "Good girl!", which I assume was directed at me, as I've heard it said about me a lot. So we got the message, okay, no peeing in the house. We know—we can only pee out the back or when we're out on our walks.

At least I thought we had the message, but then one night when they left us for the evening and Ralph was in an especially playful mood, they had left the bedroom door open. We ran riot. We had such fun, racing up the stairs, along the landing, onto the double bed, over to the other side, followed by a sharp U-turn, back onto the bed and back across the landing and down the stairs, only to jump on the sofa in the back room, off the sofa and then around the table and chairs. We must have played this game for about half the time they were out. Then, as we were racing past the table, I noticed the aforementioned yucca tree in its pot and thought, "Way hay." So we dug and dug and dug, and the soil was everywhere. And I showed Ralph how much fun it was to have a pee on top of it.

The tree (and it's a big tree, almost up to the ceiling) was leaning over because we had dug so much soil from around its roots. It was an absolute hoot. But then we heard them coming in through the front door, and Ralph and I looked at each other and thought, "Uh-oh!" I scarpered to the sofa so it would seem as though it had had nothing to do with me, leaving Ralph in the middle of all the soil. I think he was frightened, and I don't know why. He cowered and put his tail right between his legs. I had never seen him look quite so scared. When they came in, they had an odd expression on their faces, but they didn't say anything to us. Instead, they just got on with tidying up. I don't think they were very happy, and I thought maybe it had something to do with the pee, so I vowed not to do that again. And true to my word—and a grey-hound's word can be trusted—I haven't. I've been tempted once or twice to dig up that big plant again, though, but they've put some large stones in there, and I can't get to the soil, which has rather crushed that idea.

In spite of Ralph's obvious oddities, he can be a bit sly sometimes. He can be doing that coy thing, and I go to comfort him and show him how to behave. And what does he do? He jumps up on the only available soft seat in the room and makes himself comfortable. That's real gratitude for you, isn't it? Meanwhile, I have to go and inhabit the inferior dog beds over on the other side of the room. I glare at him and let him know quite categorically that it just isn't on.

I think he has been through the wars, though. I can tell that he does have a genuine fear of people, but he does seem to quite like the lady of the house in particular. He also likes the young, tall male, as Ralph lets him ruffle his ears (gosh, those ears!). He seems to be getting better with the older man of the house, the one they call Dad, and I've seen Ralph sneak up next to him on the sofa a lot lately. He also goes and lies next to him on the bed when he goes to sleep during the day, which is weird because I thought that only dogs slept during the day. Talking of which, Ralph's also quite bold at night when Dad disappears, and he's been on the bed like a limpet all day, he does the same to the female of the house when she goes to sleep at night. Up he gets, onto the bed and stretches his legs out. I tried doing the same, but it was too uncomfortable and warm with them both there, so I gave up and went to lie in my own bed where it's always nice and cool.

I feel at home here—it's so comfortable, and they more or less let me do as I want. There are some restrictions, for example, I have to wear a lead and a strange contraption that fits around my chest when I go out for a walk. However, I suppose that's a small price to pay for having people around who seem to like me. I still find, however, that when I get a little worried about things, it helps if I go and fetch Ted and wander around the house with him in my mouth. They seem to like me doing that, and they keep saying things like "Where's Ted, Peg? Find Ted!" This is all a bit silly, really, because by the time they say it I usually have him in my mouth, carrying him around by his bottom. I would have thought it was quite obvious where Ted was! It seems to keep them entertained, though. They are such strange creatures, these humans.

Speaking of strange, I've also noticed that we're not the only four-legged creatures around here—as there's an imposter. They've secreted him away in one of the upstairs rooms, but I know he's there. I've seen him gazing at me through one of his windows, and they're always going and putting tasty food in for him. He sits there and gloats at me while he puts the food in his face. Who ever heard of such a thing? What possesses a creature to push the food inside its face and then sit there looking at you when all you want is a piece of the food he's just taken? And it's there; I can see the shape of it hidden in his cheek. He sleeps all day and then, just as you're nodding off at night when the rest of the house is quiet, you can hear him and all that incessant, repetitive noise he makes as he runs and runs around on something that's in that enclosure with him. All night he goes non-stop: rattle, rattle, and rattle. All night! They give him nuts, fruit, and bits of biscuit, and all we get is dog food in a different shape to the way it is when it goes in our bowls. I don't think he deserves all those treats, not when he's just a noisy pest who stuffs his food in his face.

One morning recently, I woke up feeling ill with a very sore tummy. I'd never felt like that before, except perhaps once when I had an unfortunate visit to the animal doctor several months ago. I went in feeling well and came out with a sore part and some strange ties on my tummy. This pain sort of felt like that one had, only this time I had some horrible fluid coming from me, from right down below. I hated to do it because it smelt so awful, but I had to wash myself to keep myself clean. It was the middle of the night, and Dad let me down into the garden several times because I felt so desperate to go to the toilet. After I had been to the garden for the third time, he woke Mum, and she came and had a look at me down below. Her face changed. I couldn't work out what she was thinking, but then she stroked my head, put her face next to mine, and made that strange mwah sound.

Very soon they took me to that place where before someone had looked at mine and Ralph's ears and my leg. Once we arrived, someone put a strange tube into my other front leg, and I could see some clear fluid running into it. Mum and Dad stayed for a while and then they left me, but by then I was feeling sleepy. When I woke up, there was a sore part on my tummy and more of those strange ties. I felt sick. The tube was still in my leg, so I thought that maybe I'd try to remove it, but I was so tired I couldn't lift my head for long enough to do anything about it. Later on, when I felt like I could push myself up to stand, Mum and Dad came back for me and took me home. I was so glad to get there, as I was worried I'd never go back there again. I thought that perhaps they didn't want me anymore. I was glad to see Ralph again, and I think he was pleased to see me, too, because he did his usual leaping around like a lunatic. But then when he sniffed me, he seemed to realise I wasn't in the mood for his antics, and he left me alone.

The next day I felt much brighter and started to embark on my favourite pastime, which is stealing as much food from under Ralph's nose as possible. Honestly, that dog is just so slow at eating!

Each day I felt better and better until one day—and by this time those strange ties on my tummy had started to pull—Mum and Dad disappeared for the day. It seemed as though the one they call Anthony, the tall one, was left 'in charge' of us. He's a bit of a pushover and lets me get away with most things, but even he is getting to notice more when I steal food, which is just a little unfortunate. So, on this one particular day, when he had already intercepted me when I had tried to steal a packet of biscuits from the work surface, the bread that had been put out for the birds, and then a baked potato skin that was in the kitchen bin, I finally had my chance.

They were all distracted when Mum and Dad got home, and I noticed they had returned with some interesting bags. I pretended not to be interested, but whatever was in them smelt glorious. When that machine that they speak into made that funny ringing noise, I acted. I jumped up so my front legs were on the surface where they had left all the interesting food, and then I saw what I had smelt. It was wrapped in two layers of paper. The first one didn't bother me too much, but the inside layer was metallic. I thought I wasn't going to get it off, but then it started to peel back and reveal the most sumptuous, dark, sweet food! Then I didn't care about the texture of the paper any longer. Ralph was beside me, hovering, wanting me to give some to him, but I wasn't going to give him any. This was my find, and it was all going to be mine!

As quickly as I possibly could, I gobbled the whole lot up, including most of the wrapping.

As soon as I'd finished, there was a sudden commotion all around me. Mum was looking inside my mouth, and Dad was searching all over the floor. (Ralph appeared to be helping him.) All I could think was that if they had wanted some of that food, then they'd had it, because I'd eaten it all up.

They suddenly began to go a little wild and were dashing around the house. It was most peculiar.

I don't think I shall ever understand human beings.

CHAPTER 16

Us

Ralph doesn't really wag his tail at people. He occasionally does it to other dogs, but for a long time I didn't seen him do it to a person. I found this hard to deal with at first, as in all my years of working with dogs I had never, ever, met a dog who didn't at some point completely spontaneously wag his tail. To us, in our interactions with dogs, it's a sign that the dog is happy. I had a suspicion that he was unlikely ever to wag his tail at me when I came home, and it hurt that this might be the case. I wanted him to trust me and to like me. There were times early on when I questioned whether I was the right person for him to be living with if I couldn't make him happy. Then when I thought I didn't have any energy left to try to make him love me, I might have been sitting on the sofa reading or watching the television, when out of the corner of my eye, I would see him looking at the space beside me on the settee. I'd hope with all my heart that he'd come and sit beside me and snuggle down next to me. As time went by, he did this much more often—not just to me, but to Bob, Anthony, and visitors, too.

Whenever he sat on the sofa next to us in the early days, he would turn away from us and sit as far along the sofa as he possibly could. He would always look the other way, almost as though, like the ostrich-effect, if he couldn't see us then we weren't actually there. However, this was increasingly not the case, and as he nestled down, we could see that he was becoming more comfortable in our presence and, wagging tail or not, I really felt that we were making progress. I began to notice that when he was sleeping beside me as I relaxed on the sofa, drinking tea and reading a book, or watching television, if I reached out and stroked him down the side of his neck and onto his shoulders, he gave a gentle sigh and his toes extended upward as though he was in ecstasy. When he did this, it made me feel warm and content inside, and any doubts I had about how happy he was were banished far from my mind.

Ralph came to me at a time when my resolve was on the verge of hitting a huge slump: my dear Oskar had just died and, on that very same day my brother Martin, who has been ill for many years, was admitted to hospital and stayed there for over four weeks. Within a couple of weeks of his discharge from hospital, a family friend died unexpectedly. He was young and hadn't been ill, and the whole family and a great many other people we know, grieved his loss. He was one of those people who brightened a room and your day whenever he was around.

Amid our mourning, and with what was happening to my brother, Martin, we had brought into our lives this terrified dog who needed our love and who was desperate for the nurturing and kindness he should have received when he was a puppy.

With all our emotions in turmoil, the three of us, plus Mum (as she was staying at our house while Martin was in hospital) set about repairing the damage that had been done to this scared, timid creature. We always knew that Ralph's progress was going to be in tiny fairy steps, but with each miniscule, positive step we made, we hoped that we were enriching his life in the way that he had so wonderfully enriched ours.

At times, we'd think we'd made some progress with him, and then something would happen that would make him retreat by a few steps. For example, one morning when he realised that I was going out, he disappeared upstairs to the bedroom and lay on the bed waiting for me to say cheerio to him before I left. I reached down, approached him from underneath his neck, and then leaned forwards to kiss him on the top of his head, which is an action that, surprisingly, very early on didn't seem to frighten him. I said, "see you later," and turned and walked down the stairs. As I did so, I sensed he was behind me, following me and, instinctively, I turned around to say hello to him and made the awful mistake of reaching out to stroke him on the head. As soon as I touched him, he scarpered—straight back to the bedroom where he sat shaking.

What kind of experience makes a dog react so fearfully to an act of kindness? To pull away and run and to be so petrified all the time must be such a terrifying state in which to live your life.

We sometimes forget how nervous he can be and we become complacent, when really we should be anticipating problems. Mostly we can see potential hazards before he does, and anticipating them and acting in advance of his noticing them can help a great deal in minimising his anxiety levels. Even so, we don't always get it absolutely right. For instance, one day there were roadworks at the top of our road, and we hadn't seen them until we turned the corner. There they were, right in front of us, so we figured we had two choices: turn on our heels and go back the way we had come, or lead Ralph past the traffic cones and queuing traffic so we could get beyond the traffic lights. Feeling brave, we decided to go for the latter. Keeping a tight rein on his lead, I manoeuvred him along the path. He coped really well and I felt so proud of his achievements. I was in awe of how far he had come in his confidence.

Once we were almost past the traffic, we bumped into some other dog owners we're friendly with who were out walking their two pug dogs. Even then, Ralph stayed beside me and only jumped back a little when a double-decker bus went past. Then, mid-conversation, the pugs' owner absentmindedly reached out to touch him on the head. An innocent action all those who love dogs do instinctively, and yet to Ralph it's the one thing he just can't cope with. Just as he did to me on the stairs, he flinched away as though he had been struck on the head. When Ralph flinches, it's a significant movement, like a spring recoiling, and very alarming to those around him. You feel guilty, even though you've never, and would never, hurt him. I try to remember to tell people that he's nervous and that it's better not to touch him, but to wait for him to come to them. At least that saves everyone, especially Ralph, from any unnecessary stress.

He has taken to watching me from the living room window if I'm going off to work or to the shops. His focus is directly at me, watching me, and perhaps willing me to come back for him. There's a strong bond between us—the first few weeks he was with us he seemed only to want to be in my presence, but even with that, there's still a barrier that I hope one day I will be able to penetrate. People I have spoken to who have had dogs with similar problems have said that the time will come when he'll feel completely comfortable except—and I imagine they're right—in high-stress situations that are already so embedded in his constitution that they'll never leave him, like those sudden approaches as I've already described.

Anthony struggled with him at first as he found it difficult to bond with a dog who clearly had little intention of bonding with him. Anthony had been used to dogs who gave of themselves so willingly and selflessly. Ralph, however, very quickly came to realise that Anthony had a lot of love to offer him, and the bond was forged. As previously mentioned, we're sure Anthony's left handedness helped too.

Apart from left-handed approaches, approaching Ralph from in front of him and below his nose, right where he can see what's happening, works rather well, but to stroke him on the head when he's standing is difficult—and if there's an exit route, then he's off.

Ralph has mad moments when he goes bombing into the garden or back into the house like a crazy dog, these days taking Peggy with him—each of them jumping at each other's faces and making faux snarling noises and grumbling rumbles in their throats as they mouth at each other. Ralph has the ability to run from the front door, right through the hall, into the long kitchen, and then out of the back door, taking a leap over the three steps into the garden without touching them with his feet, landing about three meters into the garden. He then charges around the vegetable patch, usually only to be cut off by Peggy, who has anticipated his route and catches him as he comes around the other side of the garden.

He is an avid watcher of wildlife, whereas Peggy doesn't seem interested at all. He watches the rabbits that dart in and out of the bushes when we walk along the cycle paths and woods near our home. The wood pigeons are an endless source of amusement to him, and part of the reason why he races into the garden in that crazy way is in the hope that he'll see a wood pigeon fluttering up from the ground to an elevated place safe in the trees. In the interests of bird conservation, we now perform a careful visual scan of the garden to make sure there are no birds feeding before we open the door and unleash the 'lion'.

In his quiet times, he will sit for ages with his front paws tucked underneath him (very much like a contented cat pose) watching a fly, a bee, or a butterfly fluttering around the flowers and herbs that we have in large pots in the garden.

We have a hamster named Mr. Chan. He's the most adorable little creature, and yet, although both dogs spend a lot of time relaxing in Anthony's room right in the shadow of Mr. Chan's enclosure, neither dog has shown any interest in him whatsoever. This is interesting given their breeding and Ralph's insatiable inquisitiveness towards anything small and furry, or anything that flies. Unless, of course, both dogs are duping us, lulling us into a false sense of security so we'll let down our guard and stop protecting the mighty Mr. Chan.

Mr. Chan is one of the most amiable hamsters I have ever met. Anthony found him trying to escape from a tank in a pet shop. This poor creature was doing vertical leaps in the tank while flinging his whole body at the glass. All the other hamsters were milling about, getting on with their own little hamster worlds, apparently oblivious to the antics of this energetic creature. We hadn't gone in there for a hamster, just for some gardening equipment, but this 'wild' and, at that point, quite vicious, hamster made his way home with equipment and housing that cost ten times the price of him—all paid for with Anthony's student loan payment. Within days, he was the sweetest creature, and has remained so. His name is just a small reminder of the character of the hamster we collected that day.

Greyhounds are known for their gentle personalities, their desire to inhabit your sofa, and their need for little exercise. It's true that pretty much all the greyhounds we know are just like that: lazy, contented creatures who leisurely plod their way through life with the occasional short, sharp, burst of energy when they get the chance to run around a paddock...but not Peggy.

Peggy began her time with us in much the same way as I imagine every other rescued greyhound does, in that they seem almost grateful for the opportunity to laze about all day on anything or anyone they find comfortable and soft enough. And, of course, to have regular meals and a couple of walks a day. Not that they have to be grateful in any way, though, as surely it should be their right!

Peggy, at first anyway, behaved like any regular greyhound, but then she revealed her true self, because the true Peggy that had been waiting, bubbling under the surface of the quiet Peggy, is an absolute hooligan! She steals food—often while Ralph looks on in dismay—from the kitchen, the dog treat cupboard, our plates, and even my work lunch box. She races around the house like a lunatic, and she barks at you with the most high-pitched bark if anything isn't quite to her liking. For example, if we are half an hour late going for a walk or providing them with one of their three meals a day, we are rewarded with one of her characteristic 'yip's!

The dogs usually sleep in their own beds in mine and Bob's bedroom, but when he's on nightshift the dogs have figured out that there's more room on the bed. Peggy used to vie for a prime spot, but now she leaves the race to Ralph and me while she retires to the comfort of her own bed. Invariably, Ralph gets there before me and stretches out, maximising the surface area he's covering, but due to a couple of misdemeanours in the early days when he urinated on the bed and we had to purchase new duvets, we now have what we call "Ralph's giant nappy" on the bed. This is essentially a waterproof mattress cover that each morning we place over the duvet in order to protect it—just in case. Interestingly, since we started using it, there have been no little Ralphie accidents, but we continue to use it as it has the dual action of protecting the duvet during the day from those inevitable dog hairs from when we accidentally leave the bedroom door open.

Anyway, having reached the bed first, he lies there looking at me with just a glimmer of triumphant pride in his eyes, while I go about my business brushing teeth, removing makeup, putting on my pyjamas, and so on. Then I play my trump card when I go to the bed and start removing the mattress cover from over the duvet. At this point, he clambers off the bed onto the floor. Quick as a flash, I simultaneously climb up on the bed, gather up the cover, stand up (yes, on the bed), and throw (yes, throw) the cover onto the top of the wardrobe. Meanwhile, he's usually hovering at the side of the bed getting ready to jump up and claim his space. Quickly, I dive under the duvet and make space for my feet as he jumps up beside me and settles down on top of the duvet, getting ready to start his nightly ritual of stretching out his legs and gradually pushing me as close to the edge of the bed as possible. All this effort makes for an excellent night's sleep (for him anyway), while I'm teetering on the edge of the bed at great risk of falling into Ralph's own dog bed beside my side of the bed. However, I suspect that's all part of his plan—a bit like, "You sleep in my bed, and I'll sleep in yours!"

I am ashamed to say that we have become slaves to our dogs…

It is strange, though, that Ralph can have that closeness to us when we are sleeping, and yet, when we're all up and moving around he still has that level of distrust that we find so distressing. I suppose when we're sleeping, we're in a nonthreatening pose, and he feels safe with that level of contact. I guess that's also why he's more comfortable with us when we're sitting than when we're standing.

Ralph's personality is gradually coming to the fore, and when we're out walking, he trots along taking everything in. When we meet other dog owners along the way, he likes to say "hello" to the dog(s) with them. He's really friendly towards other dogs, whereas Peggy can either take them or leave them—preferably, in most cases anyway, leave them! Ralph likes it when other dogs come right up to his face to sniff him, which is the one occasion when he does wag his tail. But woe betides any dog who ignores him. Ralph does not like to be ignored and he has developed an amusing snort that he emits after he has walked past any dog who has ignored him. This snort is generally accompanied by a shake of his head, which in our human book of body language can easily be read as a snort of disapproval. Whatever it is, though, it's always accompanied by his head being held high as he trots on his way.

Not so long ago, we bumped into a man who had helped us to catch Ralph when he escaped that day. The man crouched down so he was at eye level and held his hand out for Ralph to sniff. Of course, Peggy was straight in there—in on the action, making sure she wasn't missing out on anything. But Ralph was curious too, and he leaned forwards beyond Peggy to see what was going on. With each small step like this, we feel triumphant. It's as though all the hard work with him is having an effect, that there really is hope that eventually he will emerge as a much more confident dog.

Noises, such as those from fireworks, can present numerous problems for dogs and their owners, especially if that dog is noise phobic. You can never tell which dogs are going to be afraid of firework noises. If anyone had asked me several months ago which of these two dogs would hate the noise of fireworks and become a quivering wreck if one of us didn't stay in with them around Guy Fawkes night, then I would have said without any doubt that it would have been Ralph all the way, but no, it's Peggy. We nearly caught ourselves out on 4th November by heading off for a long walk around the streets near where we live. Halfway through the walk, the noises and bright lights started. Because we had no plans to go to a display, we had completely forgotten that people might have been setting fire to some fireworks in their gardens a day early. Poor old Peg turned virtually inside out with the first explosion, and Ralph didn't even turn a hair. Yet invariably, when a car backfires, he's the one who jumps. We got back to the house as quickly as we could, closed the curtains, and put the radio and television on to block out the noise.

Ralph has a number of local 'friends' whom he loves to meet when he's out for a walk. There's a German shepherd who has the highest-pitched bark I've ever heard in such a big dog, even higher-pitched than Peggy's. When he walks past us, he focuses on his toy or whatever else he's carrying, at which Ralph inevitably gives one of his disapproving snorts. Another friend is a miniature schnauzer who lives around the corner from us. If he's not out in front of the house when we go past, then Ralph looks along his garden path. If he's not there, he goes right to the bottom of their path and lifts his leg high to 'water' the gatepost—no doubt leaving a message for the next time this mad little dog emerges from his property to survey his surroundings. More recently, he has met an old Labrador and an old Labrador cross. The old crossbreed likes him a lot, particularly when Ralph entertains her with his special rabbit dance.

Peggy is not really interested in other dogs and is more likely to offer them a sullen look or a low grumble in her throat. There's the dog we've nicknamed 'Clever Collie' because he puts all the dogs in the neighbourhood to shame with his good behaviour, which shows that you don't have to go to a breeder for a good, well-behaved, intelligent dog because he, too, is a rescue dog. Ralph tries to impress him with his rabbit dancing antics, which Clever Collie pointedly ignores—while Peggy simply ignores Clever Collie back.

Ralph has an innate curiosity towards anything smaller than him—especially cats and rabbits. While Peggy doesn't share his interest in cats, rabbits are a different matter, which is, I suppose, down to her breeding. She is generally far cooler about rabbits being around, though, and as Ralph leaps around like a lunatic trying to free himself to go and chase them (which, of course, he doesn't get to do), she looks at them quite slyly out of the corners of her eyes.

With cats, Ralph walks around his subject in an arc as though he's saying, "I'm interested in you, but not sure, and I don't really want to come too close, just in case." I think that his apprehension is wise and ties in completely with that old adage, "caution equals survival".

There's a cat who lives around the corner from us who hides himself away, ready to snarl or jump out as Ralph is passing. This has resulted in Ralph having a potentially unhealthy interest in the nooks and crannies around the hedges and walls. I think it's only a matter of time before one particular tabby cat gives him the shock of his life when Ralph sticks his nose in the hedge. Peggy has absolutely no interest in cats, and sometimes it seems as though she doesn't even notice they're there. It's as though these two dogs were almost bound—destined—to be together as they are polar opposites in so many ways. Yet, they are so needful of each other.

They get on well, the two of them. We've been very lucky with how they have bonded; especially taking into account their first impressions of each other when both of them seemed to be quite nonplussed in the other dog's presence. The deliberate age difference, which was originally intended to prevent our experiencing the same level of loss that we had gone through in the year leading up to getting Ralph and Peggy, has been a great success. This is mainly because she 'mothers' him by accepting only a certain amount of play before she lets him know quite categorically that playtime is over—usually by grabbing him around the neck or turning around and telling him off with a warning snap that says, "Okay, okay, that's enough now, Ralph!" At other times, she's as soft as putty with him, and lets him snuggle up beside her and do that thing where he reaches out and touches her feet with the tips of his toes. They really are an absolute joy to have around, and we feel desperately lucky to have found them.

We had dreaded, with a fair amount of trepidation, the meeting of Peggy with my Mum's dog, the little tearaway Luella.

Luella found herself at our local animal shelter a few weeks before we discovered she was there. Our meeting followed an email I sent to some friends who work in rescue saying my mum was looking for a small dog. The main stipulation was that the dog must be about Jack Russell size. A friend got back to me and said there was a rescue dog that had been brought over to our local centre on the ferry from another shelter in Northern Ireland. She looked very sweet in the picture on their web page, and so we arranged to take Mum to see her. Mum had recently lost her very old Border collie, so this would be quite a change for her. As Luella emerged from the kennels, we heard this almighty burst of growling and screeching and wondered what on earth was going to emerge from around the corner. However, there she was, a little larger than her picture had suggested. In spite of the noise that had accompanied her arrival, she seemed to be very sweet natured. Mum fell for her instantly, and I knew without a doubt that she would be making her way home with us once the usual checks had been done. The time for her to go home to Mum's arrived quickly.

Once home with Mum, Luella settled down really well, and they have become great company for each other. Mum spoils her intensely, and Luella has become accustomed to this and expects it. She sleeps on the bed, and she has a huge bag of treats from which to choose. This bag of treats became a bone of contention one day after Bob and I had spent six or seven hours cleaning Mum's kitchen, during which we cleared out about eight bags of clutter. Mum phoned me later on that night in a great deal of distress and, before I could even say hello, she said, "Clare, Clare, what have you done with the bag from the kitchen—the one that was hanging on the cupboard door?"

Completely puzzled, and thinking from the sound of Mum's voice that she must have lost her beta-blockers or inhaler, I said, "Which bag?"

In obvious distress, she answered, "The one on the airing cupboard door!"

Totally flummoxed, but with it dawning on me that Mum hangs her rubbish in a bag on the door handle, I answered, "Oh, you mean the rubbish bag?"

"NO!" she screeched at me, "No, not the rubbish bag; the rubbish bag was on the other cupboard door!"

"No," I replied knowingly, "there was another one on the far cupboard door. I put it in the bin." Then to confirm that I knew where it had gone, I added, "We took it to the dump on the way home."

"Noooooooooooo!" Mum screeched even louder than before. "It had Luella's treats in it."

My heart sank as I realised what I had done, and I promptly admitted that I hadn't looked inside the bag. I had just assumed that because it was hanging on the door handle that it was full of rubbish. "I am so sorry, Mum," and, thinking about her making ends meet on her pension, I added, "I'll get some more for you."

"But what am I supposed to do with her now, though?" She was obviously not going to forgive me for this, and I hadn't been in trouble like this for many years. I'm in my late forties and wasn't expecting my Mum to phone me and give me a dressing down on the telephone. I was suddenly sixteen years old again and being told off for stay-ing out later than my ten o'clock curfew. Not in any mood to let me get away with this, relentlessly she carried on. "It's Luella. What AM I going to do with her? She is absolutely inconsolable."

I found myself starting to grin at the other end of the phone and said in a flippant way—and per-haps just a little too flippant given the situation— "Well, you could always give her a human biscuit, it's not like she doesn't usually get them!"

Naturally, this made things worse, and I finally had to admit defeat and apologise for my incon-sideration of Luella's needs in throwing away her treats, even though I had had no idea in the chaos that the kitchen had been in during that after-noon that I had even touched the bag of treats. Promising faithfully that I would take Luella some treats on my next visit, our conversation ended with Mum muttering about how she'd go and find poor Luella something tasty to eat from the kitchen, and me feeling extremely guilty. Luella has since gained the nickname 'the inconsolable Luella'.

And it rather suits her.

So, with Luella and Peggy having such strong personalities, we were approaching their meeting with a great sense of trepidation. Nevertheless, we knew that it needed to be done as soon as possible or else Christmas, amid the usual cooking of the Christmas food, was going to be a nightmare. I didn't even want to consider having to switch dogs between rooms, as so many people have to in order to appease stressed relatives when the family's dogs don't get on and everyone has come together for some Yuletide joy. We already knew that we were going to have to keep Peggy away from chocolates and try to habituate Ralph to the personal challenges he would have to endure over the Christmas holiday— changes such as the Christmas tree and Christmas decorations, and generally having a lot more people in the house.

With all this in mind, and well in advance of Christmas, we took Ralph and Peggy on the thirty-five mile trip to see Mum, my brother Martin and Luella. As we approached Mum's front door, we had the usual wait while we heard the scuffle of Luella's tiny feet on the hall floor, accompanied by her familiar high-pitched bark, as she got increasingly excited about her imminent trip to the park across the road. The door opened, and she and Ralph met nose to nose and wagged their tails like crazy. They were clearly extremely delighted to see each other again.

Peggy glanced at the scene in front of her and sniffed the air. She seemed not to be interested in Luella's presence. Initially, this bothered me, as dogs can sometimes feign disinterest, like cats pretending to ignore rabbits and small furry pets when they're actually really interested in a predator-prey way. However, they met nose to nose and we took them all for a walk together. Things seemed to go rather well, with all three dogs remarkably comfortable in each other's presence. Apart from Luella's very cheeky grab at Ralph's throat as we walked down the path, which resulted in his doing one of his classic snorts and tossing his head away from her, there were no hiccups.

There isn't a single vicious bone in Ralph's body, and he would never, ever, hurt anyone or another dog. But for his nervousness and tendency to dislike people stroking him on the head unexpectedly (which would be a huge downfall in this situation), he would have been an ideal dog for visiting old folks' homes and hospices. Had he not endured the problems in life that he endured, his potential for this would have been great, as he has the gentlest nature I have ever seen in a dog.

We took them into Mum's flat, and they were fine, with them all eating treats in close proximity to each other, and the inconsolable Luella 'sharing' some of hers. At one point, just before leaving, Peggy noticed a toy we had given Luella. It's like a combined tennis ball/toy, with a tennis ball as a body, and the head, arms and legs protruding from it. Luella had shown zero interest in it, or she had until she saw that Peggy had noticed it from across the room. Peggy loves any soft toy, and this was a type of toy, which, to our knowledge, she'd never seen before. A swift intervention was necessary. I kissed Peggy on the head to console her in some way and told her the toy was Luella's. Somehow, she seemed to understand and, very quickly, especially for Peggy, lost interest in it. We headed home with their newly found dog friendships intact. Whatever was going to happen at Christmas when they were all brought together properly for the first time, at least we had given them a chance to meet on relatively neutral territory.

We had been extremely uneasy walking Ralph on the footpath outside our house ever since the day when he slipped the harness. We still used the harness, but because of his flighty nature, we had doubled up the security with a collar used in conjunction with the harness just for walking him. When he's in the house, he wears only his house collar, which is for his identity tag.

Our front garden borders a very narrow path on which you can only walk along in single file with a dog just beside you or, preferably, slightly in front of you. This is due to the closeness of the traffic as the vehicles whizz past, sometimes at a speed far greater than the thirty miles per hour speed limit. He has remained very nervous of the traffic noises. Because of this, we have minimised the length of narrow path we have to walk on by completely changing our normal walks so that we start and finish at the same point, thus only having to walk past our own house and our three neighbours' houses. Dog walks are meant to be pleasurable and, once we're off the narrow footpath, Ralph generally relaxes. However, living on a busy road is not ideal for a nervous dog and so, not thinking it was enough to merely buy a bigger car to fit our new dogs, which we had done pretty much as soon as we got Ralph and Peggy, we considered moving house to a quieter area.

We even got as far as putting our house on the market, but then gradually Ralph got better with the footpath. Because of the changes we have made to our route and the times of day that we walk, we hope he'll gradually become more confident around traffic. I think in some small way he seems to realise that the short part of the walk we do on the footpath is a means to an end, and that it is necessary to do that in order to walk anywhere around here. We love the house in which we live and wasted quite a lot of money to realise that we didn't actually want to move. I think it was just a knee-jerk reaction because of our need to take care of and nurture Ralph. At the time, I guess we were not thinking about the family as a whole.

Greyhounds and lurchers have an innate urge to chase, and therefore it's difficult to allow them to run free off lead. This is a problem where we live as they can only do it in short bursts in our current garden. They love to run and they love to chase, but to let them off in the fields beside the cycle path where we walk them would be irresponsible. They would think that every small creature was a rabbit, and if it ran away then they would give chase. One of the greyhound rescue organisers has long ago identified this problem for greyhound owners and, once we get Ralph's recall sorted out—as he needs to trust us implicitly before this will become completely reliable—has told us to feel free to use their fully fenced greyhound playpen paddock.

Some greyhound owners allow their dogs to run off lead with a muzzle on, just in case they come across a small dog or cat while loose and attack them. But it worries me that Peggy wouldn't be able to defend herself if she were attacked by another dog. Ralph and Peggy play in our back garden and have immense fun charging around after each other. Since we walk them three times a day every day, I don't think they lack anything in terms of playing and exercise.

Ralph's scar is a constant reminder of the life he had before. You can't see him without also seeing the remnants of what he has been through. I don't think he notices his scar, but he certainly remembers what happened to him because he has retained that instinctive flinch when approached from in front. He is the only one in this household who *knows* for sure what happened and, when he's in a deep sleep, he sometimes lets out a quiet scream, and pulls his front feet up towards his muzzle. Whenever he does this, we wake him because we don't want him to have to be reminded of what went on before. I believe that in the same way we relive in our dreams some of what we have experienced, dogs do, too.

There's a lovely elderly gentleman who lives around the corner from us who, whenever he sees us coming, pops back into his house and comes out with a dog treat for each of the dogs. Quite characteristically, Peggy is straight in there, gobbling her share of the morsels up in a flash, while Ralph, even though he spots this lovely, kind man from a distance, yawns a few times before he takes his treat. He still knocks it onto the ground and then picks it up from there while we hold the enthusiastic Peggy out of the way. Ralph is careful, almost leisurely, in his actions; she is bold, greedy, and forward.

And yet, in the early days when we used to go out, or were getting ready to go out, they both became absolute hooligans. In fact, we didn't even have to go anywhere for their 'parties' to start, and sometimes they were extremely blatant with their games and antics, as happened the time when Peggy stole the chocolate. She had revealed her true colours early on as a downright thief, gradually becoming bolder and bolder. Then the day she stole the chocolate, a *whole* bar of dark chocolate I might add, I just about flipped with panic.

Chocolate can be extremely poisonous to dogs, and it doesn't take as much as you'd think for a lethal dose to be given—or, as in this case and in true Peggy style, *stolen* from the work surface. She had eaten a whole 100g bar. Initially we weren't sure whether she had eaten the whole lot or whether she'd shared her yield with Ralph. For a fleeting moment, we considered that Ralph might have stolen it, but that thought didn't last for long. He is more likely to chew up Biros and pen board markers, and this? Well, it just reeked of Peggy.

Amid our panic, the telephone rang. It just happened to be the vet ringing us regarding some blood results for Peggy. She very calmly made us think rationally as we quickly diverted the conversation to chocolate poisoning. We all knew that we didn't have very long to wait if we were going to save Peggy's life.

Chocolate contains a substance in the cocoa bean known as theobromine, which is highly toxic to dogs. This type of poisoning is nasty and can result in the dog's death. Our panic was therefore justified; but thankfully for us—and many owners aren't as fortunate—this was carob chocolate and, on checking with the manufacturer, as we felt this was the only way to be sure, we discovered that the particular bar we had purchased did not contain theobromine. We were lucky, as we often have other chocolate in the cupboards and lying around the house. It was a stark warning for us to be very careful in our storage of anything similar in the future. It might not have turned out quite so well.

The vet had been ringing us about Peggy's blood results from the encounter we had experienced just ten days before the chocolate event, when Peggy was sick with a pyometra. A pyometra is where the uterus (womb) becomes infected, and if the cervix is open when this happens, there's the obvious sign of a pus discharge coming from the bitch's vulva. It wasn't a true pyometra though, as she had been spayed six months before we got her.

There was a lot of pus that Sunday morning, and as a veterinary nurse, I knew what the discharge was likely to indicate. Knowing that she had been neutered, I had a strong suspicion that she could have an infected uterine stump, which is sometimes hormonal and sometimes caused by a reaction to the suture material used in the original spay operation. The discharge had an awful, extremely offensive smell, and she was clearly not well, even though the day before she had been frolicking around like her usual lunatic self.

Off to the emergency out-of-hours surgery we went. After waiting with her and comforting her while she had some intravenous fluids and a scan of her abdomen, we stayed while she had her sedative and then left her with the veterinary surgeon and the nurse from the practice. She had to be opened up again so they could see exactly what was going on. We went home where I spent much of the day in tears, snuggling into Ralph and hoping we'd have Peggy back soon. We had only had her for such a few short months, and she had got under our skin and become a part of our family, and we loved her unconditionally.

Later on that day, we picked up our poor old wobbly Peg and took her home. The diagnosis had been confirmed, and knowing what we were dealing with calmed my nerves. My heart filled with joy when she and Ralph met again back home. They were so pleased to see each other and, in spite of her obvious tenderness around her abdomen, they touched noses, and she wagged her tail.

The following day you would never have imagined that this crazy greyhound had been through major surgery, because it took us all our efforts to calm her down and prevent her from doing herself an injury.

Peggy was back.

Winter

CHAPTER 17

Rescue dogs

The long winter nights provided me with ample quiet time to embark on a mission to find out more about where Ralph had come from. Staff members from the rescue shelter where we got him were only able to tell us that they had taken an urgent call from a shelter a couple of hundred miles away. He had been a stray who had reached his time up and, unless somewhere had been found for him to go, he was going to be euthanised.

Following my success in finding out so much about Peggy's history, I trusted the Internet and put in a search for his name and some other details I knew about him. That's as easy as it was to begin the trail of finding out more about this mixed-up dog who'd found his way into our hearts.

He had, indeed, been on the verge of being put to sleep, and I discovered that in desperation someone had posted a message asking for some-one, or a series of people if necessary (as eventually became the case) to transport him to the no-kill shelter. It stated that he could be a little skittish sometimes but that he was lovely and was just in need of patient, gentle handling. They got his character in a nutshell really, didn't they?

It went on to say that he had arrived with a flea infestation that had been rectified. Then in the punch line—there on the World Wide Web for anyone to see—were the words that he was 'at risk of being put to sleep'.

He really was that close to not being rehomed and I guess that, but for the dedication of a series of people along the way who were prepared to give up their own time to transport him the couple of hundred miles to his safe destination, that's what would have happened to him. Euthanasia is easy— sometimes too easy. There are too many dogs and not enough good homes, and while uncontrolled breeding continues, that will remain the case.

I got in touch with one of the people who had been involved in his rescue. I suppose I hoped that she would know more about him. But here was the surprise: many of those people who were instrumental in saving him had never even seen him. What an amazing, altruistic group of people. Even in rescue shelters when you are working with animals, the job is tough, but you often have the reward of seeing those big, soft eyes, having the dog lick you in apparent gratitude, or seeing that ever-rewarding wagging tail.

We feel so overwhelmed by his story and that he found his way to our local shelter where we were the people who became lucky enough to be able to offer him a home.

Animal shelters are packed with animals that have been bought on a whim —pets so often having been purchased to make a family complete or as a reward or pacifier for a child. Then all too soon, the family realises they were complete already; or the child loses interest in the animal. They are sometimes bought to fix a family but, in time, the family realises they are beyond fixing, and the dog or cat ends up in a shelter or is euthanised...while the family falls apart.

If they're lucky, the animals that reach the shelters are found a good home, these days termed a 'forever home', indicating that the dog, cat, hamster, rabbit, or horse will never again be exposed to a life without someone there to feed, clean, exercise and care for them. This concept of rescuing an animal penetrates something deep in our subconscious and invokes in us a need to nurture that is satisfied, at least on some level, through sharing our life with another species.

People who love animals dearly, and who don't see them as a mere commodity or a way of making money, are the ones who have to pick up the pieces and fight what can feel like a never-ending battle against the cruelty that goes on amid the never-ending supply of dogs and cats (and horses, rabbits, small pets and reptiles) that find their way into the pet market. When working in this environment, it is so easy to feel that you are banging your head against the proverbial brick wall, and you can lose your faith in human nature. When you're presented daily with a constant stream of dogs and cats that are healthy strays, injured strays, or those brought to you by their owners because they no longer want them, your heart can sink through the floor each time the phone rings or a door opens and yet another homeless animal is handed to you. People who take their animals directly to a shelter do deserve some respect, however. At least they have had the guts to take the animal somewhere where they will be safe, rather than abandoning them to an unknown fate.

There are also the animals that you HAVE managed to rehome who later come back to you as cruelty cases or strays. Years ago, I was involved in nursing a longhaired dog, who was initially presented as being very underweight with fur that had completely matted around his poor, skinny body. However, we restored him back to really good health and he was rehomed. We all happily waved him good-bye as he went off to start his new life.

Several months later, that same dog came back to us as a starved, extremely matted dog. It transpired that his new owners had been no better than his previous ones. This was not a one-off situation. When I worked in rescue, I became less and less optimistic about people's intentions and wondered about the plight of some of the animals that were being rehomed. Where were they going? Would they be happy? Would these owners treat them well? Were they going to be the type of owners who were more interested in whether the dog's colour matched the wallpaper than its health and wellbeing? This was not an easy situation for me to deal with emotionally and was one of the reasons why I realised that, for me anyway, being directly involved in finding homes for animals was not something with which I felt comfortable.

Don't get me wrong. There ARE some really good homes out there—in fact many, many really good homes. I'm sure the good ones outweigh the awful ones, but the pet industry is swamping the market with so many animals that these good homes are too few and far between. This is not a brand new twenty-first-century problem because it has been like this for several decades and, to my mind, the only answer is for something highly radical to happen towards change, and that's to neuter, neuter, neuter, and chip, chip, chip every dog or cat that enters any rescue organisation. This is starting to happen, but progress is often too slow.

In addition, I feel it is vital to strictly control the number of litters a bitch or queen is allowed to have before neutering is enforced, and to ensure that those animals' offspring are chipped, and new owners are encouraged to have them neutered once their new pets are old enough. If all dogs and cats had to be identichipped at the time of neutering or vaccination, then it would go a long way towards helping the situation. Animal charities all over the world are working extremely hard towards this goal, but where breeding becomes a massive, uncontrolled enterprise, as in the case of puppy farming, these dogs are further saturating an already saturated situation.

If the animal shelters are anything to go by, it doesn't matter whether you're a Chihuahua, a Lhasa apso, a Great Dane, an Irish wolfhound or a humble mongrel, your fate can be just as desperate as the next dog's, and animal homes and breed rescue organisations are brimming over with pretty much any dog you fancy. If a person likes a particular breed, then it is often worth checking these organisations to see whether there is a dog of that type (or perhaps a lookalike!) in need of a home.

My heart sinks when there's a new blockbuster film that has highlighted a particular breed of dog, because you can predict that the particular type of dog shown will become the latest craze. Years ago, the latest fad was for people to go searching for a dog who was shown in a particular TV series. I won't say which one, for fear of causing another craze, but let's call him 'Joey'. So many people phoned or came in saying they wanted a Joey-dog, and did we know where they could find one?

Bemused, we told them to try the local animal shelter, because Joey just happened to be a mongrel!

With a little effort and patience, most people would be able to find their ideal dog in a shelter or through a breed rescue organisation. There are already so many dogs and cats needing a home that, until we have the current problem resolved and a high proportion of the homeless animals homed, the Staffordshire bull terriers, Border collies and Labradors which have already saturated the system, won't have the chance of finding some-one to adopt them.

Many people decide that they want a puppy or kitten, rather than an older dog or cat. They have the idea they will be able to bond with it more easily and believe that they are easier to train. The majority of adult dogs are just as easy to train, however, and they have so much to offer. As for bonding with them, although they might not be as cute as puppies, the puppy is very shortly going to become an adult dog. They offer unconditional love whatever their age or size, and it is easy to reciprocate their love. Like dog shelters, those that house cats are absolutely over-flowing with adult cats that need a good home. And yet, all too often, people are more attracted to the cuteness of a kitten. I understand that some families may prefer a young animal that can grow up with young children, but if there's no real preference for breed, then shelters have puppies, too. And there may even be the surprise attached to what the puppy is going to end up looking like!

Shelter dogs can sometimes arrive with a mixed bag of issues—some quite mild and others, as with dogs like Ralph, that are a little more problematic. Peggy arrived with a fear of people walking towards us when we had her out on a lead, but this was easily rectified by showing her through food (of course!) rewards that those people were not a threat to her. Luella had a fear of being alone and had some kind of superiority complex towards other dogs. Both of these problems have eased with the affection she has received. Ralph came with all his neuroses, and we are unpicking his problems little by little—one tiny miniscule emotion at a time. And, gradually, his confidence is growing.

All three dogs came with a distinct lack of house training, and this was easily sorted with all three of them. House training should only very rarely present a long-term problem; it is something that comes naturally to dogs, as they don't like to defaecate or urinate in their den. By giving them a lot of opportunities to go outside and rewarding them when they go to the toilet in the correct place, it should take only weeks, not months or years. Yes, there will be the occasional accident, but these will be rare if the hard work is accomplished in the beginning.

The neurotic aspects of their temperaments take much more time to conquer, but you work through the problems they have, and they're a challenge, but then one day you look at them and you see what you've achieved together. You hope that they're happy and that it's all been worth it for them, because there is no doubt that it has been rewarding for you. And you take pleasure in each tiny step along the way.

Some people make a lot of money out of breeding dogs and, for many (not all), that's what it's about—financial gain. Many breeders are enthusiastic about their particular breed and want to protect the line, and I do appreciate that, but the problem in hand needs to be dealt with by all those who care for dogs and their place in our society. Breeders vary considerably in how they approach the rearing of their dogs' offspring and, in many cases, these dogs are born in kennels and don't ever see the inside of a house. They never hear a washing machine or see a set of stairs and for seven or eight weeks their lives revolve around a wooden or brick-built shed, a concrete run, and the sounds of other dogs barking and howling. All this, combined with the presence of their highly stressed mother, whose natural instinct is to protect and nurture her babies.

When the right age arrives for going to a home, they emerge from their sheltered, barren lives as dogs who are poorly socialised and incapable of dealing with life in an outside world that includes children, people of all ages and sizes and, in most cases, other animals. I believe that Ralph, while not a pedigree dog, was such a dog. Bred for the purpose of chasing hares, and probably rabbits, he has a timid state of mind that has resulted in his lack of confidence. This, coupled with extremely poor handling, and probably cruelty, at the hands of someone in his past, has made him an example of one of the many problems we have today with our relationship with 'man's best friend'. We owe it to them, after all these thousands of years of having them as our companions, to put these problems right and to rectify all the mistakes that we have made.

In spite of always having used kind, gentle methods, I have made mistakes in my training, socialisation and habituation of dogs in the past. Most people do—it is very difficult for anyone to be right about everything—especially as every dog is an individual with his own personality. However, as each year goes by you become wiser. In the last couple of decades, attitudes towards training have changed, with, thankfully, most people now using and promoting kind methods and trying to work with dogs that in the past would have been euthanised. With each dog, you become more knowledgeable and better tuned in to their needs, and you hope that you are doing right by them.

People often ask us whether our dogs are rescue dogs. I guess they are, but not rescued by us, as we only gave them a comfortable home, plenty of walks, and lots of nice food. The rescue part is jointly to the credit of the organisations who took them on each stage of their journey. This was the journey that culminated in their pictures being posted on the web pages, which subsequently found us browsing through the images with the emptiness in our hearts from the loss of our old dogs. Seeing the dogs who needed to be loved, we wanted to contribute in some small way to the plight of homeless dogs. I hope in a way that it's like a butterfly effect, in that for each dog who is rehomed, a space becomes available in an animal shelter. Then another dog can try his or her luck at looking out from the pages of a charity website and appealing to the heartstrings of another person who might, just might, offer a loving home.

I feel that those taking on an animal for the first time should have some form of assessment before they are allowed to do so, and while this has been helped in recent years by the increased scrutinisation of potential owners through home checks and so on, I feel more could be done. Perhaps a questionnaire about dog behaviour and training that you have to pass before you're allowed to take a dog home would help.

I have seen so many disastrous dog-human combinations, and when listening to owners talk about how their dog lives and how they treat their dog, a part of me wants to scream out, "But you're doing it wrong! Your dog doesn't enjoy spending eight hours a day alone in a crate (cage) in your kitchen, or alone outside in the garden in a kennel while you are working. He doesn't understand you when you talk to him in long sentences and you wave your hands about in front of him. He hates it when you don't have him on a lead, and he runs across the road or across a park or field to "speak" to another dog, and you catch up with him and tell him off (or worse, hit him) for running away. All that tells him is that when you catch up with him, he's going to get hurt. Would you go running up to someone who was meant to care for you if you knew they were going to hurt you?"

Dogs like their owners to be tuned in to how they're feeling, and here I am in danger of being accused of anthropomorphism. But they have emotions that mimic ours, and they are sensitive creatures that over many thousands of years have become tuned in to the feelings and idiosyncrasies of humans. Domestication has changed them from their wolf origins, and they have become a very different species.

People may say that there are so many human problems going on in the world, so why do I get so cross about this one? Well, I care about those human problems too, but I also believe that the human-animal bond is an important part of our time here on earth. If we get this one right (and it is one that can be resolved a lot more easily than some), then it will help us to solve some of the others. Our association with animals helps to humanise us, to make us kinder towards them and towards each other. We need to chip away at all of society's problems, and as so often one problem is embroiled with another—for example, the association between dog fighting (or hare coursing), violence, and gambling—the effects of solving one issue can help to solve others.

So, returning to the story in hand, and with Christmas approaching, the three dogs we had brought into the heart of our family earlier in the year seemed oblivious to the chaos that was about to disrupt their lives for a few days. We didn't know for sure where they were last Christmas, but we were determined to spoil them even more than usual over the festive period. The only snag was that in spite of our having several weeks before done 'The Big Introduction' to Luella, there was a little niggle in the back of my mind (which every now and again in the time leading up to Christmas had manifested itself as a lurch of panic in the pit of my stomach) that Peggy was this large, predatory type of dog who had been accustomed to sprinting around a track after a mechanical rabbit. Luella, on the other hand, was a small, rabbit-sized, rabbit-coloured terrier who liked to be in charge of everyone and everything in her midst. They had met only once, and the entire time they had been restrained on leads.

Not the best combination for a peaceful Christmas!

CHAPTER 18

Christmas – Us

My brother Martin is on kidney dialysis, and so the timing for collecting him and Mum to come and spend Christmas with us was fairly critical, as it had to be on Christmas Eve after his late-afternoon dialysis session at a renal unit forty miles away.

Having collected Martin from the hospital and Mum from the Christmas Eve service at her local church, we had the two of them packed into the back of the car, surrounded by some of their luggage, which we had built carefully around them. Heaving a sigh of relief that we were finally on our way home for Christmas, we plonked Luella in the back of the estate car with the rest of their luggage and closed the boot lid. In that childlike way, I felt a rush of excitement that all the preparations were finally complete. However, that's when the festive scene developed into one of complete chaos.

Not one for being excluded from the action, and always wanting to be the centre of attention, Luella had clambered up on top of the luggage in

A DOG LIKE RALPH

the boot and, in one swift movement, scaled the dog guard and landed on Mum's shoulders.

Now, Mum's an elderly lady, and having even such a small dog land on top of her is no great joy. However, Mum is also an avid crisp eater and, at the time this happened, she was searching through her bag for the packet of crisps she'd put in there for the journey. While hell broke loose all around her, all she could think about was where the crisps were. While my brother was trying in desperation to find the aforementioned crisps for her, Bob and I were trying to get Mum to sit in the front of the car so I could sit in the back while holding onto the incorrigible Luella. This mean feat took no less than twenty minutes, while Luella was screeching at the top of her voice in protest at the possibility of having to go back behind the dog guard, and Mum and Martin were having an increasingly heated discussion about the where-abouts of the crisps.

Eventually, with me secured on the back seat nursing Luella, and Mum in the front passenger seat nursing her crisps, we headed off on our way. My optimism of less than half an hour earlier was waning and, as we drove along, that familiar sinking feeling about Peggy and Luella entered my stomach.

Once home, we kept all three dogs on leads and allowed them to reacquaint themselves with each other. To unite on neutral ground, we took them for a walk and then headed back to the house. Once there, it became apparent very quickly that as he had been before, Ralph was going to be fine with Luella, even if she was being particularly grumpy with him, so we let him off the lead to mingle with her.

His freedom restored, Ralph seized the opportunity to dance around in front of Luella, simultaneously baiting her for a reaction and wanting to play with this dog he so clearly thinks the world of. Characteristically, Luella was having none of it and up came her lips as she flashed her tiny white teeth at him. Ralph backed off and tossed his head in that way he does, which in human terms can only be defined as a 'couldn't care less' shrug, and went off to his toy bucket to find a toy to play with instead.

Due to the size difference, Luella was the next to be allowed off her lead, and she flaunted her leadlessness in front of Peggy and Ralph, making a beeline for the sofa so she could elevate herself above the two of them. Peggy stood up straight and looked at her eyeball to eyeball, and we tightened the lead, just in case. We had seen the size of Peggy's teeth, even if Luella had not yet noticed them.

Peggy looked away. We were unsure whether she was feigning disinterest or if this were genuine, so we decided to keep her on the lead a while longer until we were sure, especially as her ears were forward in the position that was typical for her if she spotted a white bobtail bobbing down the cycle path before it dived underneath the hedgerow.

After a couple of hours, and when the dogs seemed reasonably settled, we took a deep breath and unleashed Peggy into the sitting room.

And they were fine—to a point anyway. Ralph did his usual prancing around, which appeared to have become especially elaborate considering his new position in possession of his very own 'harem'. Peggy lay quietly looking out for signs of anything that could be classed as a treat, or at least had the potential for becoming a treat with a little coercion in the direction of whoever was in its possession (or, failing that, just stealing it). According to Peggy, if it's edible, then get it by whatever means—even illegal ones. Meanwhile, Luella guarded Mum's side, waiting for either Ralph or Peggy to dare to venture anywhere near.

The one danger I anticipated was the chase factor. If we let the dogs out into the garden, there was the danger that if Luella ran, then quite instinctively Peggy would momentarily forget that Luella was a dog. I'm sure that she had realised this but, seeing a small brown flash, she could dart after her to do what all greyhounds wish they could do to the mechanical hare: tear it to shreds. The thought had flashed across my mind several times over the weeks leading up to Christmas, and having anticipated it, I wanted to remain in control of the situation and prevent anything from escalating. Hence, any visits to the garden involved our letting Peggy and Ralph out and keeping Luella on the lead. All was well, and very smugly I thought to myself, "So far, so good."

In hindsight, however, my smug thoughts were a little premature.

On unhooking Luella's lead at the back door, Luella was delighted at her sudden freedom, and she darted back into the sitting room to take up sentry duty beside Mum. On seeing the brown flash race past her, Peggy gave chase and was on Luella's heels as she jumped on the sofa. With the might of a gnome brandishing a machete, Luella turned quickly and snapped at Peggy. And Peggy, in retaliation by this point, opened her mouth and flashed those giant canines of hers. There was a screech of alarm from Luella, and Martin grasped hold of her collar and pulled her from Peggy's closing jaws. It was a close shave, and I'm sure that Luella saw the depths of the cavern of a black hole at the back of Peggy's throat. However, this close encounter seemed to draw a line in the sand, and Luella and Peggy, on the face of it anyway, appeared to settle down. Nevertheless, the real truce didn't come until Christmas morning.

Bob was on nightshift and he disappeared at about ten o'clock on Christmas Eve, while the rest of us finished getting Christmas ready and took it in turns to be on dog observation duty. Finally, at midnight and feeling quite exhausted, I climbed the stairs and collapsed in a heap under the duvet. With sleep not far away and Ralph already snuggled on top of the bed, I breathed a contented sigh of relief that I could finally go to sleep.

Unfortunately, Peggy had other ideas.

Over the years, Mum has developed a routine of around a hundred and one things that she has to do before she can get into bed, and this routine stops for no man, and certainly not Father Christmas. As she can't manage the stairs, Mum was sleeping downstairs. Peggy's acute hearing, and the fact that she saw Mum as the most likely target for getting her paws on treats, meant that Peggy, on realising that Mum hadn't yet gone to bed, had decided that even though it was a quarter past midnight, it was okay for her to come to the side of the bed and bark at me with that piercing, high-pitched "yip" of hers. I turned over and tried to ignore her, but it was no good. The high-pitched yip became a loud bark, followed by her bounding over to the bedroom door to wait for me to open it.

Still worried that she might mistake Luella for a rabbit, I held onto her collar and took her downstairs to show her that, actually, no one was getting any treats. And then, just in case she really had wanted to go to the toilet, I let her into the garden—at which, she just stood outside the back door looking back in at me.

Taking her by the collar again, I led her back upstairs, put the light out, and nestled into the pillow.

I could still hear Mum mooching about downstairs and considered putting on the radio to try to drown out the noises emanating up the stairs. Within seconds, from across the room I heard a soft whimper. I lay as still as I could, hoping that she'd settle down. Then the whimper became louder, until she let out another piercing yip and came and deposited herself at the side of the bed, right next to my ears, each shrill noise increasing in decibels. I made the mistake of going, "Sshhhh," in the hope that she'd get the message, but then because she realised I was awake, the barks got louder. By this time, it was around one in the morning, and all I could think about was my poor neighbours, who were probably fast asleep waiting for Santa to arrive. Very reluctantly, I got out of bed again.

'Frog marching' her down the stairs, through the kitchen, and into the garden, I was getting extremely cross. "Look, there are NO treats, and NO ONE is having any biscuits, any chews, or anything else tasty. They are having NOTHING!" She clearly didn't believe me because, as I reached the bottom of the stairs for the FIFTH time and realised that it was nearly half past one in the morning on Christmas Day—and that neither Mum nor Peggy seemed to be any closer to getting into bed—in desperation I let out some kind of inhuman, primeval noise at the top of my voice. I then carefully, slowly, walked to the back door and stood there feeling strangely numb. I listened to the chimes that were in the garden as they gently chimed against each other and composed myself. Peggy looked back in at me, clearly wondering why she *still* hadn't been given any treats.

Whatever language had been emitted from my lips in my desperate frustration due to sleep deprivation seemed to have worked, and finally Peggy got the message. So she and I returned upstairs to our respective beds. Ralph, who very early on in our nocturnal adventure had decided he was *not getting involved,* was lying curled up right in the middle of the duvet. Nudging him over enough so

I wouldn't have to cling to the edge of the mattress all night, I eased my way under the duvet and finally got to sleep.

When Mum woke up at six-thirty, Peggy made it clear it was time to get up. She and Ralph bounded down the stairs ahead of me. They were clearly very excited at having extra people and Luella in the house—and it was absolutely nothing to do with whether or not Santa Claus had visited during the night.

Present opening went without any hitches, so I started to relax. The three dogs had their own new toys and at last, in Peggy's mind, some treats, but we remained aware that the dogs still hadn't really established themselves together as a group. When clearing up after opening the gifts, we had an unexpected turning point in the dog dynamics in the house, one much more powerful than the whole 'meeting on neutral territory' method of introducing dogs to each other. Whether this will make its way into dog training manuals, I doubt very much, but the turning point in the bonding of these three dogs came when the three of them united against a common enemy: the vacuum cleaner!

It was as though the fear of the vacuum cleaner being pushed noisily around the sitting room was something they had in common, as they all hated it with a passion. And they hated it so much more than any grievances they may have had with one another.

Therefore, in many ways, the vacuum cleaner became a turning point in the events for us, too, in that we became much more relaxed. That much calmer attitude continued to have a knock-on effect on how the dogs were feeling. So, by the time Christmas evening arrived, Luella had quite happily lay sleeping on the sofa, first of all beside Ralph and then, much later on, beside Peggy. She still had grumbles at them, but they showed no signs of retaliation, with Ralph simply tossing his head away from her and Peggy just ignoring her. I'm sure that, in the end, there remained no doubt in her mind that Luella was indeed a dog and not a rabbit.

Very sensibly, on Christmas night, I waited to go to bed after Mum had done everything she needed to do. Whether Peggy was tired because of the excitement of Christmas, or whether it was because she had kept me up the night before and remembered our encounters (which is the theory I like more), or perhaps because I'd had the sense to wait until there was no mooching about downstairs, we all slept like logs. I woke up on Boxing Day feeling much more refreshed than the day before.

On Boxing Day, we took Mum home, as she's not one for staying away for very long, and I sensed with Ralph and Peggy that they had enjoyed their time together as a group of three. I'm not so sure about Luella, though. I think she likes having Mum all to herself and that she appreciates being able to be in charge of taking up sentry duty at her side so she can guard and protect her from the evils of the world without any interruption from the likes of Ralph and Peggy.

We had survived Christmas. In the days that followed, we were thrilled with the apparent progress that had become evident in Ralph in terms of his level of confidence. He started to greet us more enthusiastically and come to us more willingly when called. Even with visitors, he developed a sense of being much more curious about them and approached them voluntarily. We finally saw real progress and a true hint of the dog he was becoming. He started to get excited when he encountered new things, and it became a real pleasure to see his reaction when he greeted something or someone for the first time.

With it being Christmas, lots of people had 'SANTA PLEASE STOP HERE' posts in their front garden. This was something we'd thought of getting in the past but never quite got around to buying. Well, it seems as though we shall have to get one for next year, and it absolutely must be one with Rudolph on it, for some neighbours on the next street had one, and it was positioned on a pile of gravel—and Ralph loved it. We think that when he first saw it he thought it was a rabbit because there are quite a few rabbits that dart around in that area. He saw it and became transfixed on it and, where at first he approached it with caution, he would then dance around it, waiting no doubt for some kind of response from it. Even though there was clearly no response forthcoming it didn't perturb him, and he leaped up and down like a lunatic. We can only guess that he thought a rabbit was sitting there, motionless, staring at him. You'd have thought that when he realised it wasn't actually a rabbit, he would have lost interest in it, but no, it was the most exciting thing he had ever seen.

And so there I was just a couple of days after Christmas, sitting with my two dogs lying comfortably next to me on the sofa, and a steaming cup of tea warming my hands. I had just read on a networking site about a spaniel cross that had been left tied to a fence near to an animal refuge. There was no note left with him, he was not identichipped, and there were no other clues about where he had been in the time leading up to his being found by someone from the rescue shelter. However, the truth is that he had been *somewhere*. He had been in *someone's* possession over Christmas. I only hope that he found a home and that his new owner is better able to understand his needs.

CHAPTER 19

Christmas – Ralph

And there she was.

She had come to visit me.

That little dog with the teeth and the big attitude was standing at the bottom of my steps with her shoulders high, obviously trying to make herself look bigger and more frightening. Well, it was working because I wouldn't argue with her, and it was unlikely that Peggy would either, although I have to admit I was anticipating that not long after the dog with the teeth arrived, there was going to be trouble—and I mean Trouble with a capital T!

Well, there I was minding my own business and having something to eat in the place where they make the food, when, out of the corner of my eyes—and I can see quite a long way around each side of my head—I saw a brown ball of fur race past me. "Uh-oh," I thought, as the streak of brown was followed closely by a streak, and a much larger streak at that, of black. I followed behind to have a look at what was going on. There was a bit of commotion as the little dog shrieked and raised her lips back further than I had ever seen them go. Peggy opened her mouth wide and I could just see the little dog's eyes nearly bulging out of her head as she was pulled away from Peggy's jaws. "Phew, that was a close one," I thought to myself. Peggy retreated and I was relieved. I don't really like too much aggravation going on around me.

It was time to put on our jackets and loops and head off into the cold, windy, dark night for our walk before bed. As we approached the corner, and my ears were flapping in the wind, I started to feel a sense of excitement in the bottom of my body. I hoped it would still be there. It had been there on every walk for some time, and it was such fun. It stood there with its big ears, just like those creatures, and I wanted to play with it. When I first spotted it, I had thought it actually was one of those creatures with the ears. Then I realised how silly that was, so I yawned at it a few times to see what it would do. It didn't do anything. The time after, when I saw that it was still there, I was almost beside myself with joy, but still it didn't move. So I raced up to it and tried to make it move, and still it didn't. It just sat there looking at me. After that, I always jumped towards it and tried to make it move, but it never did.

But it was great fun trying.

I showed it to the dog with the teeth and Peggy, but they didn't seem interested in it. In fact, Peggy gave it a disinterested sidelong glance, but that could have been because that's the way her eyes look at things. The dog with the teeth didn't even glance in its direction. I didn't understand them because it was great fun. They just didn't know what they were missing.

In the time before the dog with the teeth arrived, things had been a little hectic at home. Mmm seemed to spend a lot of time putting things in containers and wrapping them in lots of paper, and then a tree appeared in the window. This was on the same day that they wrapped some bright, sparkly stuff around Peggy's neck. I thought at first it was a new fancy loop, but they didn't put any around my neck, which I was actually quite relieved about. Really, I don't think Peggy was too pleased that they put it on her. In fact, when they turned their attention back to the tree, Peggy managed to escape from it. They picked it up and put it on the tree, which I thought was very strange behaviour indeed.

The tree had lots of twinkling lights on it and round ornaments that twisted and showed the light when there was a slight breeze in the room. Sometimes I liked to stand and watch it and see if there was anything I could take off it, but they said, "No, Ralph." I know that means I shouldn't do something, so however much I got tempted, I just left it alone and yawned at it instead.

Apart from the strange tree in the window and lots of wrapping of things going on, there was also strange goings on in the kitchen with them making lots of food. A variety of different sweet and savoury smells drifted through the house. However, the weird thing was I didn't see them eat any of it, not until a few days later anyway, when they never seemed to stop eating. Peggy and I were totally flummoxed by this. Why would you keep food hanging around the place when you could eat it right there and then?

The whole house was in chaos when the dog with the teeth arrived, and eventually we all went up the steps to where we sleep and left the dog with the teeth downstairs with the woman that smells of the white sweets. I say "we went to bed," and certainly I did. I darted up the steps, launched myself onto the top of the big soft bed, and nestled down for the night, as it looked as though it was one of those nights when the man was not going to be there, so there'd be plenty of room for me to stretch out.

So, there we were, Mmm under the big, thick cover, me sprawled on top of the bed, and Peggy lying in her bed, which was next to my empty one. And then Peggy started to whine—very quietly at first, but it got louder and louder—until she walked across the room and barked right next to Mmm. She wanted to go down the steps because she could hear the old woman and the little dog. I'm not sure what she wanted to go down for, but Mmm took her. I waited for them to come back. I think Peggy was hoping she'd get a biscuit, but she didn't. Instead, she went back to her bed and let out a big, long breath.

So we settled down for a second time, and it wasn't long before Peggy started again. Mmm took her back downstairs and still didn't bring back any more biscuits. Well, you'd have thought that Peggy would have got the message, but it kept on happening. Each time Mmm got more and more cross, until the last time it happened, when she threw the cover back off the bed (which I thought was a bit extreme as I was quite cosy) and went and got Peggy by the collar and took her down the stairs. I think Peggy realised she'd gone too far, especially when I heard Mmm make the strangest noise with her throat. When she brought her back upstairs, Peggy went back to her bed and stayed there until morning.

There were still no biscuits though.

The next day everyone seemed really excited, and when the man came home from where he sometimes goes at nights, they all sat around. And do you know what they did? Well, it was so strange, but they unwrapped all those parcels they had previously wrapped up in paper. The human world is a strange one. Why wrap them up if you're only going to take the paper off again?

There we were surrounded by all that ripped paper, when some more parcels arrived. They smelt of the bags they sometimes bring home that smell of the treats and biscuits they give to us. They crouched down in front of me, Peggy, and the dog with the teeth and opened them. Inside there really were some treats and, not only that, some toys, too! Well, Peggy and I were beside ourselves. Peggy had this bright yellow bone-shaped thing and a soft toy that she was parading around, trying to keep them away from the dog with the teeth. The dog with the teeth didn't seem to be interested, though. She had this round toy that had some kind of material wrapped around it, which she was guarding, and she clearly didn't want the yellow bone. I had been given a shoe-shaped toy and one of the soft, fluffy toys—the same as Peggy's. I yawned at the shoe a few times because I could tell it wasn't a real shoe and, to be honest, I didn't really know what to make of it. I think I still prefer real shoes—especially Mmm's shoes that I always pull the inside out of. This new one had an inside, but you couldn't pull it out easily, which kind of took the fun out of it. Later on, I discovered that the fluffy toys made a noise when you bit into them. They were great fun, especially when Peggy got the other end of one and tugged at it.

The Peggy versus the dog with the teeth saga continued, but I think they both decided to keep a respectful distance from each other, with Mmm and the others keeping a close eye on them. Then something happened that forced them to confront the fact that we were all in the situation together.

There's a cupboard under the stairs where the monster is kept. It's this huge machine, which, for some reason I can't quite fathom, they get out of the cupboard each day and push around all the floors. Well, once the parcels had all been opened, the man went to the cupboard. I thought to myself, "Uh-oh, time to retreat," and disappeared under the table in the room where the sun shines, as I've realised they don't seem to take the monster under there very often. Peggy hasn't realised this, though, so every time the monster appears, she keeps on dodging past it as it chases her through every room. I've also discovered that it's quite safe to stay up high on the big seats, but you have to be brave to stay there as you can still see it coming to get you. So, Peggy and the dog with the teeth charged around the house being chased by the loud monster, while I stayed under the table, waiting for it to go back into the cupboard.

Safe at last, I gingerly came out from under the table. And well, what do you know, there's Peggy and the dog with the teeth, standing in the place where we have our food, waiting for the man to give them a biscuit. Needless to say, I went and joined the queue, politely taking the biscuit when I was offered it; unlike the other two, who snatched theirs out of the man's hand.

For the rest of the day, the people ate a lot and watched the noisy box in the corner, and then the next day the dog with the teeth and the old woman went away again. I think Peggy and the little dog had come to an understanding by this time: Peggy wouldn't go near the old woman or the dog with the teeth's ball toys, just so long as the dog with the teeth didn't get any extra treats.

It was a strange few days. I saw a lot of people and went on a lot of walks, and I feel less scared now, as no one's hurt me here. I don't think they will, but there's always something in the back of my mind, a little niggle that I have to remain on my guard. Just in case.

CHAPTER 20

Family

I would love to get behind those almond eyes of Ralph's, to be able to sink into them and experience the world as he does and see what he sees, instead of how we think the world appears to him. He suffered—we know that, and we won't ever know what he went through. Whatever it was, he has retained it in his psyche. His fear instincts are so ingrained that, even with all the love that we can give him, we know that he'll still, even years from now, sometimes shy away when we reach out to touch him. More and more frequently nowadays, he forgets the distrust and we find him allowing us to greet him properly, as greeting is still the main problem. When that happens, the experience pulls on the strings of my heart as I snuggle his head with mine and inhale that wonderful, comforting, doggy smell.

Just the other day, Ralph wagged his tail at Bob when he returned from his night shift. Our hearts melted as this was a huge triumph. Ralph had finally started to confront his greatest fear: that of men.

He is definitely better, and he thinks the world of Anthony. With Bob, he gets better and better as each day passes. For instance, if Bob is sitting on the floor in front of the sofa, Ralph will often go and lie next to him, completely voluntarily, and lie with his head across Bob's feet.

He's safe now and I want to do everything in my power to keep him and his best friend Peggy safe from harm for the rest of their lives. There are so many dogs out there, just like Ralph, Peggy, and Luella, who need loving homes. If those who want to give a dog a loving, understanding home were more likely to consider a dog from a shelter, and if identichipping, neutering, and registration of dogs became a legal requirement for owning a dog, then the dog crisis we have would be better under control.

I hope that Ralph and Peggy are happy here. I think they are, and I know that we shall always do our best to consider them in everything we do to keep them comfortable and healthy. Even so, there's always a little niggle that perhaps we could do better. I know they'd appreciate a much bigger garden, and so would I, but it's not practical at the moment, although it remains in our long-term plans. With their three walks a day, I don't think they miss out on the exercise front. At weekends, on days off, and during holidays, we take them into the hills and forests for extra-long walks, which they seem to appreciate. Ralph sometimes doesn't like strong winds as they make his ears flap, and he hates the rain, but Peggy is like some intrepid explorer, loving every second of her adventures, whatever the weather.

Ralph has changed. There's a new side to his nature, almost as though he feels safe now, and so much more relaxed and contented. He loves toys, and he plays happily with Peggy or us. I think that on many levels we have conquered whatever happened to him before. He snuggles on the sofa next to us and doesn't deliberately turn away from us anymore, and these days he's not particular who he sits next to, visitors included, indicating that his fear of men is so much less. There's a sense of cheekiness about him that wasn't there before, and he applies some of the play antics that he has always used with Peggy with us, too, as he prances about and play bows. The two of them together are a joy that, in the early days, I would never have imagined to have been possible.

Peggy is beautiful. From a distance, she looks just like any other black (with a little white) greyhound. She has the most adorable, sweet face. However, I'm sure that others who have black greyhounds would say the same about theirs, too! She is greying around her muzzle, and this has become more obvious throughout the last year. Perhaps it is living in our busy house that is making her feel old. She is very clearly middle aged, and she's much more intelligent than greyhounds are usually given credit for being. She communicates her thoughts to us very willingly through short, sharp vocalisations, which we interpret as "I'm hungry; feed me," "Time for a walk; take me out," or "It's bedtime, and time for my treats." These barks are usually directly into our faces from about two feet away, and we usually get the message and obey.

Luella, in spite of her very domineering character, is extremely affectionate and really keen to learn. She, too, is going grey around her (very small) muzzle, and I suspect that she's actually a little older than we thought—although greyness is not always a great indication of age, as you only have to look at most black Labradors that go prematurely grey to see that. Luella has found herself a great companion in Mum, and Mum thinks the world of her. Luella has made sure that a small part of the heart of each of the rest of us has been reserved for her, too.

And so, I guess this book is not like your average dog story, which, in the majority of cases anyway, culminates in the inevitable eventual demise of the main canine character. That's what we've come to expect following years of dog stories that have been adapted into blockbuster films, stories that are designed to make even the toughest of hearts melt. But this is not the story of their whole lives—it is simply the beginning of what we hope will be long and happy lives as part of our family.

These three very different creatures have enriched our lives, and I hope that we have enriched theirs. I hope that the experiences we will share in the years to come will become the stories of the future, and the bonds that we have forged will remain in our hearts for as long as we live. If there is another life after this, then I hope that our lives will remain entwined as they are now.

I suppose all that's left to be said can be told by a couple of the stars of the story themselves...

This is the world according to Peggy and Ralph:

Peggy lies on her back with her legs in the air—I don't know how she does that. It's almost as though she has some kind of magnetic force pulling them up. She lies down, rolls onto her back, and zing! Up they go, straight into the air. Then her mouth opens and her lips fall back revealing those huge teeth of hers. It's no wonder the little dog with the teeth decided to back off. I think I would as well if I saw those fangs coming at me.

Ralph still yawns at the weirdest of things, and I just can't fathom him at all—either he's tired or he isn't, you know? What is it with the yawning thing anyway? Yawn-stretch he goes, yawn-stretch, and then he pauses and goes yawn-stretch again. I tell you it's infectious because he has me doing it now. In fact, when we get up in the morning, we stand at the side of the big bed. He goes yawn-stretch, then I go yawn-stretch, and we keep on doing it several times. I think he's some kind of exercise freak.

I still feel unsure of myself at times, and yawning gives me time to think about my next move. Peggy didn't used to do it much, but she does it all the time now. At first, I thought she was mocking me, but I think she's doing it now to show me that everything's really okay.

Ralph occasionally prances in front of me and tries to nip at my face when I'm trying to have a snooze on the sofa. I put up with it to a certain extent, but then I tell him, so he runs off. Then of course I have to chase him! Mum and Dad tell him

"No, Ralph," too, and he's getting the message. He never actually makes contact, and I know he's just an overgrown puppy. But still, he's incredibly annoying.

Peggy is sometimes not much fun, and I have to dance around in front of her to make her chase me. Mostly I dangle a toy in front of her; other times, the only thing that works is if I play-nip in front of her face and dodge back out of the way in case she catches me with those gigantic sharp teeth of hers. Sometimes she gets quite cross with me, a bit like she does when I nip at her in the garden to try to get her to chase me. And that's exactly what she does. She chases me, snapping at me with her big mouth, and we run around the house until someone says, "Peggy, no. Ralph, no." Then we calm down a bit.

Ralph hasn't realised that when he's on the lead it's nigh on impossible for him to catch the creatures with the ears and that it's better to ignore them. Recently he developed this strange fixation with a sign that was sticking out of a pile of stones, and I'm sure he thought it was one of the creatures. However, if that was the case, then why didn't he just leap on it and catch it? His behaviour had become embarrassing, especially when he did that over-exuberant rabbit dance of his every time he saw it. In the end, I chose to look away each time we walked past the sign; I just couldn't bear to watch. It's gone now, though, thank goodness.

Peggy is not interested in the creatures with the ears, and yet you would think that with those long legs she would be able to chase them. She wasn't even interested when I spotted that creature with the ears that was sitting quite blatantly on top of the stones. It didn't move for ages, so I started to doubt whether it really was a creature. But now it's gone, so it must have been.

Ralph steals Ted and tries to run off with him, but I'm faster than he is, so I catch him and snatch Ted back from his grasp. Sometimes he tries to pull Ted's insides out, and I'm ashamed to say that sometimes I help him. However, mostly I take Ted right back and put him in another room. I was given a big yellow bone recently, so I've started to carry that around instead. At least 'Bone' doesn't have any stuffing, so Ralph can't tear him open, but I'm ashamed to say that we *have* chewed the end off him.

Peggy won't share Ted, and every time I pick him up, she snatches him out of my mouth. Ted has the most amazing fluffy stuff inside him, which, if you tear him, you can pull out and spread all over the floor. I don't think that Mmm and the man are too impressed when we do that, though, as they pick it up and then get the monster out of the cupboard to push around the floor.

We like to drink out of the birdbath together, and sometimes Peggy even lets me start to drink first, which is very nice of her. Sometimes the flying creatures are feeding in the garden, and I race from the back door trying to catch them, but they're too fast for me.

Ralph comes and hassles me when I'm having a drink from the birdbath and, reluctantly, I stand aside and let him drink next to me, as that's much more pleasant than him splashing me while he drinks. He tries to catch the birds, but he's stupid even to think he'd be able to catch them. I don't know whether he's noticed yet, but they have wings and can move in the sky, and he doesn't.

She's really greedy and seems to be quite obsessed by food, for example, sometimes she steals treats from right under my nose and is so quick that I often don't get a chance to get to them before her. Then when we're having our proper food in our bowls, she starts hers, and once she's done she comes and helps me to clean my bowl. I don't mind really, but when I go to look at her bowl, there's hardly any left, so I lick the remnants in the bottom and then go back to my own bowl, and she's usually finished it for me. I say "for me," but I guess it's really "for her"!

He nips at my bottom when I'm walking in from the garden, and actually this is probably his most annoying habit of all, even more so than when he does it in front of my face. So as much as I like him and everything, sometimes I turn around and nip him back. However, Ralph being Ralph, he thinks this is all part of a big game, and it makes him worse!

Peggy doesn't like it when I try to get her to play by nipping at her bottom, and sometimes she turns and nips me back. Then I'm not sure whether she actually liked it in the first place and was only pretending to be cross. This makes me do it even more, but then Mmm, the man, or the tall one, calls us back inside and spoils all the fun.

My favourite times are when everyone is together and we all relax in front of the noisy box, and Peggy lets me lie next to her on the sofa. I like lying next to the humans too, but Peggy's more comfortable because she has fur. Sometimes when I have bad dreams and thoughts of what went on before come back to me, it's comforting having her close to me because I think she understands. We have dog beds too, but the human ones are the best.

Ralph doesn't mind anymore when I rest my head on his back when we're on the sofa. I love it when we all sit around, we've got full tummies (as the full tummies are especially important), we've had a long walk, and it's nice and cosy and warm. Sometimes when he's resting, he twitches, and I think that whatever it was that made him the way he is must have been bad. If we're lying together on the sofa, then I press in closer to him and let him know that he's okay now.

I'm glad Peggy came to live here with me.

I'm glad they brought me to live here with Ralph.

We're glad they came to live with us.

The End

However, I suppose, with being a terrier (of sorts), Luella will insist on having that final, *absolutely final*, last word…

"Well, the next time they come to visit, they had better bring some dog treats with them, or I'll be absolutely inconsolable and have to sort them out once and for all. Big teeth or no big teeth!"

Thanks

There are so many people I need to thank for their advice and help throughout my writing of this book, and they all know who they are, but thank you in particular to my dear friends Pat, Elaine, Catriona, and Emma for reading my words and giving me the advice (and the occasional kick up the backside) that I needed. Thanks to Bob and my Mum, both of whom also read them and gave me feedback and encouragement. To Jan, Rose, Cassie and Debbie, I know you would have read it, too, if I'd asked, but I knew you had other things going on at the time.

To the rest of my family, thank you for your support, help, and patience—I love you all very dearly. To Bob and Anthony, in particular, you are both my rocks and much of what I do I couldn't do without your love and support.

To the design and editing teams at Createspace – thank you. You took my work and polished it for me. I am utterly grateful!

I have changed the names of some of the characters in this book. Those people will know who they are, and I want them to know that I am wholly grateful to them for the parts they have played in this story, and for the roles they played in rescuing Ralph and his compatriots, Peggy and Luella. Many of you are innocent bystanders who were pulled into the story by default—right place, right time, and always the right motives...

And to Ralph, Peggy and Luella
Without you three, there wouldn't have been a
story...

Two years on...

Busily getting on with their lives as part of our family, Ralph, Peggy and Luella have nominated me to be the one to give an update on how things have been for them since they last felt compelled to 'voice' their opinions...I say "busily getting on with their lives", but in reality what that means is that Luella is far too busy keeping a check on anyone who dares to cross her path, Peggy is spending her leisure time lying on her back sleeping on the sofa with her legs in the air, seemingly without a care in the world, and Ralph? Well, Ralph has discovered there's a family of wild rabbits living behind the garden shed, and he sits gazing out of the French windows utterly fixated on any sign of movement so he can bark at us to let us know they're in the vicinity...

The bond between Peggy and Ralph is almost impenetrable. She continues to be everything we ever hoped she would be to him—friend, playmate, comforter and mother-figure. To her, perhaps, he is the puppy she never had? She has an over-exuberant passion for soft toys and constantly carries them around in her mouth, presenting them to you, but also taking care of them and collecting them from around the house—almost as though they are her offspring. Perhaps this goes some way towards explaining her behaviour with Ralph. Although she is neutered, since we got her she has endured a multitude of visits to the vet for gynaecological problems, some of which have resulted in hers and Ralph's temporary enforced separation for a day or two. It is difficult for both of them—Peggy because (like most dogs) she hates going to see the vet, and even more so having to undergo surgery; and Ralph, because he hates it when she's not around.

Years ago, when I was working as a student veterinary nurse, there were two dogs who used to come in together for regular check-ups. While living abroad, their owners had found them wandering as strays and taken them into their home and cared for them. These two dogs were probably related because, although they were crossbreeds, they were very similar to one another. When circumstances forced their owners to move back to the UK, they couldn't bear the thought of having to find them a new home abroad, so they brought them over with them. This meant the dogs had to undergo six months in quarantine. Six months is a huge chunk out of a dog's life, but back then, we didn't have the benefit of pet passports.

Therefore, these two dogs spent six months in quarantine together, and their owners visited them as often as was allowed. When these two dogs emerged from quarantine, the bond between them was far more solid than the bond between any dogs I have ever encountered. They could never come to the surgery without both of them being there, and one couldn't be examined on the table without the other jumping up on the table beside him—and they were at least a good forty kilograms each! Together they would sit patiently waiting for whatever would happen next. Peggy and Ralph's bond is close, but they don't like the vet quite enough to take it that far! Since having Peggy and Ralph, though, I have often thought about those two dogs.

During one of Peggy's recent encounters at the surgery, she needed another general anaesthetic, and had to stay there for the day. On her return, Ralph was beside himself with joy to see her and bounded over to her wagging his tail and emitting his characteristic "Rowff" greeting, only to be rewarded with a warning growl. She was clearly not quite in the mood for his enthusiasm at that moment...but it didn't take long for her to get better. She doesn't stay down for long when she's poorly.

We took them both on holiday to a small cottage in the northeast of Scotland. The stairs creaked so much that neither dog would go up them, so we had to create a 'Hansel and Gretel' style trail of tasty dog biscuits all the way up to the landing. It worked – most dogs will do anything for food. We spent the holiday walking the cliffs and tired them (and us) out. When you take your dogs on holiday with you, you have a different style of holiday in that it's more of a self-catering walking holiday than sitting on the beach basking in the sun (an unlikely occurrence in the northern parts of the UK anyway). On one of our walks along the shoreline we saw a familiar shape in the distance—another greyhound!

It's amazing how dog-people are drawn to one another. While we verbally pondered over the joys of having a rescued greyhound in our lives, the dogs seemed happy to be in the company of another dog similar to them. We all wondered aloud, though, how do they know the difference? Do they really recognise other greyhounds? Perhaps it's that definite slender shape? The other dog's owners had moved from the continent to the UK just months before and this regal-looking dog (she was very beautiful), in the same way that our two have for us, had made their lives complete.

Now, greyhounds are not really known for their intelligence—their design is for speed, not logic. If someone wants a truly intelligent dog, they couldn't really go wrong with a collie (of any type or cross) or, strangely, a poodle. Perhaps I should emphasise, greyhounds *are not known* for their intelligence, and yet, every now and then, you see a spark that makes you think that perhaps the dog world is doing greyhounds an injustice!

One day as I was putting the dogs' food into their bowls, Ralph and Peggy stood beside me, waiting patiently. Once I'd placed it in the bowls in their raised food stands, Ralph began enthusiastically eating his, but Peggy made it quite clear that she was NOT going to eat THAT flavour! She looked at me, back to the bowl, back up at me, and then back to the bowl again—trying as hard as she might to break my resolve. Deciding I was not going to be browbeaten by her, I turned away from her, fully expecting her to start eating it.

She didn't!

I slowly turned my head around so I could see what she was doing, and her eyes were boring a hole into the side of my head. Realising she once again had my attention, and with her head held high, she marched past me to where the dog food is kept. She promptly picked up a packet of dog food of a different flavour. As I looked on in astonishment, she marched back to me and placed it down on the floor in front of me.

Extremely impressed, but still not wanting to give in to her, I said, "No Peggy," pointed at the food in her bowl and went to pick up the packet she'd put on the floor. Before I could get to it, she picked it up and ran past me towards the sitting room, whereupon she plonked it on the floor and started to gnaw at it to try to open it.

She won!

Dutifully, I took it from her, went into the kitchen and emptied it into her bowl – with a little bit of it for Ralph, of course!

Intelligence? I'm not sure, but there's definitely something going on between those ears of hers...

When we're out we continue to have adventures with cats and wild rabbits—especially cats! There's a cat we have named 'evil-cat', who lives not far from the people who have the Santa Please Stop Here sign (people who, last Christmas very kindly bought Ralph his own sign, just like theirs). This cat is definitely in charge of not just his own household, and the dog he allows to reside there, but the cul-de-sac he lives in *and* the adjacent street. When 'evil-cat' is around, Ralph cannot take his eyes off him – just in case he moves towards us. However, moving towards us would be too obvious a thing to do for this cat, as instead he sits and glares at any dog who dares to walk down his street. Not just dogs, though, also cars. We have seen this cat sitting in the middle of the road emitting his evil-cat-glare causing people to have to drive past him to get to their own homes. Anyone who invades his patch gets that cold stare— I bet he's a real joy to treat when he visits the vet!

Luella and Peggy seem to, at last, have drawn a truce. While we are still quite careful with them when they are together, there seems to be a mutual respect for one another. Luella's personality is such that she is still very 'dominant', and I suppose she is not dissimilar to 'evil-cat' in that respect. When she goes for walks in her park, with the emphasis on *her* park, it is clear she believes wholeheartedly that she is in charge! Other dogs, large or small, avoid her, and she lets out a grumble at them when she passes them on the path. One beautiful, friendly collie came bounding over to say "hello" to her one day and he got the 'treatment', so immediately he did a U-turn once he was ten feet away, and went bounding back to his family. Occasionally she will say "hello" nicely, but that's much less of a frequent occurrence.

While she *thinks* she is in charge when she is out for walks, when she is with Mum, there is no doubt whatsoever who makes all the rules. And it's not Mum.

It appears that Lucy has acquired a taste for drinking tea. On challenging Mum about this and informing her quite categorically that dogs do not need tea, dogs should not have it as part of their diet, and that tea is just, well, not dog food, Mum answered, "Well, it's okay because she doesn't like sweetened tea—she prefers it with milk and no sugar!"

For once, I was speechless, however tempted I was to point out that adult animals do not need to drink milk!

While Luella has this apparently tough exterior, on the inside she is like any other family dog. She loves food, treats, walks, to play, and most of all she loves to be cuddled. She continues to be a great companion for Mum and I know that Mum thinks the world of her...and despite of all our grumbles about her domineering character, the rest of us all have our own little soft spot for her.

And so, eventually we took the plunge and decided to move house. Despite loving our old home, and the idea of leaving the house and all its memories behind pulling on our heartstrings, we wanted more space. We realised we needed somewhere we could throw a ball for the dogs. The bonus of leaving what was an extremely busy road has meant that Ralph is now more relaxed and walking him is much easier. We never quite let down our guard, though, and every now and then, we venture onto busier footpaths so he doesn't forget that the world out there isn't all like this quiet place where we've moved. We need to know that when we take him to see the vet, on holiday and so on, that he will be able to cope with crossing roads.

The first time we let Ralph and Peggy loose in the new garden, Ralph raced around making footprints in the frosty grass, and seemed in his doggie way to appreciate what we had done. Peggy, on the other hand, seemed to have a much more laid-back attitude and appeared to say, "Well, look guys, this is very nice and all that, but when's dinner?"

These dogs have altered our lives in more ways than we could have ever imagined, and we feel so lucky that they are here by our sides...

Ralph

Peggy

Luella

Books by the same author

Lilac Haze: Love, loss and hope

You don't remember your childhood in detail, so your memories thirty or forty years on have become hazy; times you had back then are painted in colours that have become distorted, and you find yourself recalling conversations you have created in your head.

Through living in the false world of remembering, you can deal with the past in such a way that the things that happened, they appear to matter less.

This is a love story.

In the end, anyway, that's what it will be.

A love story gives you hope: whatever you have lost; whatever you have to gain. For me, as someone on daily kidney dialysis, when an offer of a kidney came along which I couldn't possibly refuse, there was everything to gain.

But the past has a way of interfering with what seems as though it is the right path... and how do you ever in this life repay a debt so huge?

A Soldier Like Jack

Like millions of other young men, Jack was plunged into a war which was to change his life, and the lives of his loved ones, forever.

While his brothers left Britain to fight in France and Belgium on The Western Front, Jack's war would take him to Salonica (Thessaloniki), in Greece.

This book paints a picture of the world as seen by Jack's wife, Grace, who tells the harrowing story of what happened to the men and the families they left behind. It traces their lives from the time of Jack and Grace's marriage in 1912, until Grace's death in 1957.

This is a true story based on the lives of the author's great grandparents, Jack and Grace Cogbill.
The book reflects the lasting impact of war on the families of ordinary service men.

If you have five minutes, please get in touch and let me know what you think of my books. You can contact me either on Facebook, or through my web page:

clarecogbill.com
*
I'd love to hear from you

Made in the USA
San Bernardino, CA
23 August 2018